Foreword

In the last century, we saw clear distinctions between the physical and the digital world. We have chipped away at these barriers with technologies in networking, unified communications, cloud, Big Data and analytics, social, mobile and of course the Internet of Things. The result—a confluence of traditionally inanimate objects tied to sensors and analytical ecosystems. In fact, every device enabled by a sensor and tied to a network takes us closer to the convergence of atoms and bits.

This transformation is analogous to the early days of social networking through peer-to-peer networks. As more people entered the networks, each individual gained from the collective insights from all the clicks, likes, transactions and interactions. The network effects create a massive treasure trove of data that ties back to information. The information piped into business processes and customer journeys provides insights that can be surfaced. Each of these patterns surfaced and questions answered creates additional intelligence to ultimately drive decisions. We can now take data and democratize decisions through these networks of people.

In parallel, the Internet of Things has occurred at geometrical scale. Constellation Research, a Silicon Valley-based analyst firm, predicts over 80 billion sensors powering Things by 2020. Consequently, objects will talk to each other and gain network effects. The intersection of where objects engage with humans drives an unlimited set of possibilities for customer experience, smarter machines, healthcare, trading networks, fraud detection, transportation and other use cases to be discovered.

Thingalytics is happening now. Market leaders and fast followers are in the midst of this digital transformation. As organizations transform and create new business models and cultures with digital technologies a distinct set of winners and losers will emerge. Success will require organizations to invest in new technologies that not only complement, but also abstract older technologies. These technologies must deliver on mass personalization at scale and deliver in the right time context and real-time speed. Context- and intention-driven design are expected and not a luxury.

Digital Darwinism is unkind to those who wait. This brave new world of smarter machines, and the humans who engage them, will change every industry and every market segment. Today's digital divide serves as a precursor to the impact of Thingalytics. The top three competitors in every mature market segment control 43 to 71 percent of the market share and 53 to 77 percent of the profits. Thingalytics represents this next evolution of digital disruption. Savvy leaders should take note on how to disrupt first or face disruption.

R "Ray" Wang (@rwang0)

Principal Analyst and Founder, Constellation Research, Inc.

R "Ray" Wang is the Principal Analyst, Founder, and Chairman of Silicon Valley based Constellation Research, Inc.

He is also the author of the popular business strategy and technology blog "A Software Insider's Point of View." With viewership in the 10's of millions of page views per year, his blog provides insight into how disruptive technologies, and new business models such as digital transformation, impact brands, enterprises, and organizations.

Thingalytics

Smart Big Data Analytics for the Internet of Things

DR. JOHN BATES

Thingalytics: Smart Big Data Analytics for the Internet of Things

Copyright © 2015 by Dr. John Bates. All Rights Reserved.

For information about this title or to order other books and/or electronic media, contact the publisher:
Software AG
Uhlandstr. 12
D-64297 Darmstadt
Germany
www.softwareag.com
John.Bates@softwareag.com
Twitter: @drjohnbates

ISBN: 978-0-9897564-2-6

Printed in the United States of America

Cover and Interior design: Luke Johnson

Wang has held executive roles in product, marketing, strategy, and consulting at companies such as Forrester Research, Oracle, PeopleSoft, Deloitte, Ernst & Young, and Johns Hopkins Hospital.

He is a prominent and dynamic keynote speaker and research analyst working with clients on digital, innovation, business model design, engagement strategies, customer experience, matrix commerce, and big data.

His Silicon Valley research firm, Constellation Research, Inc., advises Global 2000 companies on the future, business strategy, and disruptive technology adoption. Ray is a regular contributor to *Harvard Business Review* and well quoted in *The Wall Street Journal, Forbes, Bloomberg,* CNBC TV, Reuters, IDG News Service, and other global media outlets. Wang has thrice won the prestigious Institute of Industry Analyst Relations (IIAR) Analyst of the Year Award.

Wang's new book *Disrupting Digital Business* will be published by Harvard Business Review Press and will be globally available in the Spring of 2015.

Thingalytics

Introduction

Q. What is Thingalytics?

A. Thingalytics is the use of real-time analytics and algorithms to make sense of the fast Big Data arising from the Internet of Things.

People often ask me: "John, what really is this Internet of Things? It sounds like a lot of hype about smart fridges that tell you when to buy milk."

Actually, the Internet of Things (IoT) is much more important and transformative than that. In fact, it is going to change everything—just as the original Internet did.

We've all heard about innovations like self-driving cars, which are now a reality (although not yet approved for mass use). Consider the next step: In the future all cars will communicate with one another, as well as with smart roads and smart cities, to coordinate and optimize journey times—and avoid collisions.

Likewise, we are all familiar with the mobile smart phone, and we are starting to see more wearable devices like smart watches. We are now on the verge of experiencing the next generation of wearables, such as heads-up-display glasses that communicate with a location-aware "smart cloud" that can tell you if you have friends nearby or send you special shopping offers and interesting restaurant ideas—perfectly tuning this "augmented reality" to your behavior patterns and preferences.

Until recently these thrilling innovations were widely dismissed as science fiction. Today, however, they are becoming—or are close to becoming—reality. At the grassroots level, smart Things come to life by using sensors and actuators, which are then attached to networks, thereby enabling us to monitor and control them remotely. This new universe, made up of these networked smart objects—or "Things"—is called the "Internet of Things."

The Internet of Things is about digitizing everything in the real world and integrating it into the Internet. In some cases this technology is new; for example, washing machines that we can control remotely and that can message us when a wash cycle is complete and alert us when they are about to break down. In other cases it has been around for a while; for example, digital data from the stock market that we can stream, enabling us to place our trades electronically. The Internet of Things brings together this existing digital streaming data (stock market, news, weather) with social media (Twitter, Facebook), along with new sources of data from real-world objects.

> **The Internet of Things is about digitizing everything in the real world and integrating it into the Internet.**

Real-world objects are "digitized" by capturing their status using sensors. Different types of sensors can track myriad factors such as temperature, location, pressure and speed. Upload those sensor readings onto the Internet, and any appropriately authorized app can consume, analyze and respond to them. Put an application programming interface (API) on the object, connected to onboard actuators, and suddenly the app can control the object remotely.

People also ask me: "Is absolutely everything connected, and if so, then how can we possibly keep an eye on it all?" They may even suggest: "I'm not sure I want to be monitored or probed, so back off." And so I do. Promptly.

The idea of the Internet of Things has come to the fore as technology has become more capable. As the costs of sensors and connectivity drop, viable use-cases are increasingly realized. Put simply, the Internet of Things represents an emerging reality where everyday objects and devices are connected to the Internet, most likely wirelessly, and can communicate

> **Where this gets really interesting is when we think about a multitude of Things working together, like a swarm of ants collaborating on a common goal.**

with one another at some intelligent level. Where this gets really interesting is when we think about a multitude of Things working together, like a swarm of ants somehow collaborating on a common goal.

As for the scale and growth of connected Things, there are many predictions. The analysis from Cisco, the company that wants to be the connector of the Internet of Things, is shown in Figure 1. Cisco estimates that by 2008, the number of Things connected to the Internet was close to 7 billion. To put that number into perspective, it exceeded the total number of people on earth.

Cisco further estimated that in 2015 the number of devices hit 25 billion and by 2020 this number will double to 50 billion. In 2015, the ratio of devices to people is 3.5:1 and will rise to 6.6:1 by 2020. In addition, the market research firm International Data Corporation (IDC) predicts that by 2020 the Internet of Things market will grow by more than $5 trillion, exceeding $7 trillion. The number of Things and the data volumes they generate are mind-boggling. As we'll explore in this book, a whole new type of software architecture is needed to support Thingalytics.

Every mobile phone call, smart watch reading, Facebook update, connected home heating adjustment, and smart car trip generates a new piece of data. The result is massive clouds of data, all of which are interconnected. As both the volumes and the velocities of data continue to increase exponentially, many firms are struggling to scale their existing infrastructures. Going further, firms have to re-imagine how they do business—leveraging the Internet of Things to become more competitive.

Modern businesses require new, agile systems to handle the computational explosion of sensory inputs and reference data generated

Everything (and everyone) is connected 24/7

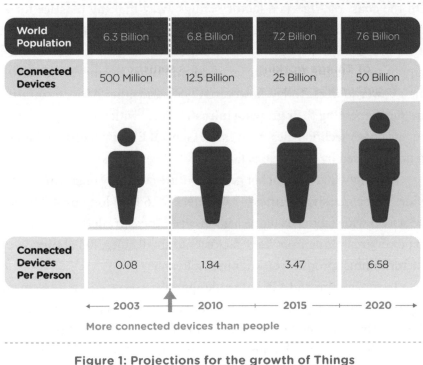

World Population	6.3 Billion	6.8 Billion	7.2 Billion	7.6 Billion
Connected Devices	500 Million	12.5 Billion	25 Billion	50 Billion
Connected Devices Per Person	0.08	1.84	3.47	6.58

2003 — 2010 — 2015 — 2020

More connected devices than people

Figure 1: Projections for the growth of Things
Source: Cisco

by the Internet of Things. Thingalytics is all about collecting the right information, analyzing it in the right way and driving the right decisions to make systems smarter and even self-learning.

The IoT becomes very exciting when we see how lives can be saved, fraud avoided, customers delighted and carbon emissions reduced. It gets scary, however, when we realize that a single mistake can mean millions of dollars lost in seconds, company reputations ruined in moments and lives put at risk. In this book we explore how to enable the opportunities of IoT while avoiding the threats, by presenting pertinent use-cases such as the following.

Predicting the Future

On the coast of Algeria a factory chugs away making plastics for its customers, secure in the knowledge that its electricity won't conk out. It was not always so. Algeria's domestic energy demands often outstrip supply, making it difficult for factories and other businesses to rely on their power sources. Today, however, Algeria and other African countries are supplementing their growing infrastructures with natural gas-fueled, on-site power technologies, such as the General Electric Jenbacher[1] power generator used by the plastics factory.

Roughly 11,000 Jenbacher generators are currently operating worldwide. These massive engines—8.4 meters (27.6 feet) long by 4.7 meters (15.4 feet) wide (about as big as a good-sized travel trailer)—can be used to power everything from large factories to small cities. Reliability is key: Factories must produce; cities must be livable.

To achieve this end, GE has made aggressive service-level agreements (SLAs) for these engines. In the event of a failure, engineers have to get the machine serviced and back in action within a specified timeframe. And—even more of a challenge—these engines should experience only a very limited number of breakdowns. In fact, the objective is a 99.999 percent uptime from each engine. This is tough to achieve!

The trick to ensuring that a machine is always up and running is not to wait for it to break down, but, rather, to fix it before it breaks down. This is a difficult task, however, because Jenbacher engines are used in a variety of ways; for example, some run at a constant rate, whereas others experience peaks and troughs of heavy and light usage. If you could constantly monitor the usage, then you would know exactly what could go wrong and when. And that's exactly what GE does.

---

[1] http://www.businesswire.com/news/home/20140805005988/en/GE%E2%80%99s-Distributed-Power-on-Site-Technologies-Supporting-Algeria%E2%80%99s#.VLaJMSvF9SE

Bill Ruh runs a lesser-known division of GE—GE Software[2]. His mission is to make GE's customers' systems 1 percent[3] more efficient. One percent doesn't sound like much, does it?

In fact, a 1 percent fuel reduction in power generation equates to a savings of $66 billion over 15 years for GE's customers. This is not a trivial sum. Significantly, GE's equipment is already highly efficient. So, how do they improve it?

The answer is that Bill's department monitors the behavior of the Jenbacher machines by using smart systems software that includes 300 sensors that are reviewed continuously. The department analyzes and visualizes the data and compares it to predictive maintenance rules over time. They use smart analytics to determine when a generator bearing will wear out or malfunction, or how much life is left in a sparkplug—at any point in time. It is this increase in efficiency and uptime that will generate the 1 percent improvement.

When Algorithms Go Wrong...

Early on the morning of August 1, 2012, a tiny piece of code nudged an automated trading system into action on the U.S. stock market. As trading began, the rogue command triggered a buy order for 140 different stocks on the New York Stock Exchange (NYSE). In a frenzied buying spree, Knight Capital Group's trading platform scooped up shares in companies ranging from General Electric to the semiconductor company Spansion. Spansion's stocks changed hands at least 4 million times—all in the space of 45 minutes!

---

[2] Bill Ruh, VP GE, October 10, 2013: Keynote presentation Software AG Innovation World.
[3] John Gertner, Fast Company, July/August: "Behind GE's Vision For The Industrial Internet Of Things." http://www.fastcompany.com/3031272/can-jeff-immelt-really-make-the-world-1-better#10

What happened? Subsequent investigations revealed that Knight Capital had installed new software[4] that conflicted with old code, which was supposed to have been deleted. The clash caused a flood of orders to surge onto the NYSE, without the benefit of volume caps.

By the time the trading firm realized that its system was wreaking havoc on the marketplace, the rogue trades had dramatically pushed up the value of many stocks. Because Knight's capital base had been sucked dry by the buying spree, it had to sell the overvalued shares back into the market—often at a loss. This single piece of errant code had cost the company around $440 million, or roughly $10 million *per minute*! The losses sent customers fleeing to other trading companies and tripped a torrent of selling in Knight Capital shares, wiping out 20 percent of the company's value in a matter of hours and leaving the firm's market capitalization below the amount of losses it had sustained.

Knight Capital teetered on the edge of insolvency as its executives desperately sought funding from "white knights" from other business sectors[5]. Four days after the debacle, the company was saved by a consortium consisting of Getco LLC, Blackstone Group LP, Stephens, Inc. and Jefferies Group, Inc., as well as Stifel and TD Ameritrade, which put together a $400-million rescue package.

How could a trading company fall from the lofty peaks of success and respectability into the chasm of imminent bankruptcy in the space of less than an hour? Today's super-fast algorithms and high-speed electronic trading systems rule global markets, and errors such as Knight Capital's coding mistake can move markets—or even take down a firm—in a matter of minutes.

---

[4] John McCrank, Reuters, October 17, 2012: "Knight Capital posts $389.9 million loss on trading glitch." http://www.reuters.com/article/2012/10/17/us-knightcapital-results-idUSBRE89G0HI20121017

[5] Michael J. de la Merced and Nathaniel Popper, NY Times Dealbook, August 5, 2012: "Knight Capital Reaches Rescue Deal With Investor Group." http://dealbook.nytimes.com/2012/08/05/knight-said-in-talks-to-obtain-new-capital/

So what did we learn from Knight? The Internet of Things will feature super-fast algorithms that make real-time decisions. Capital markets is just one example; everyone makes mistakes, and algorithms that make decisions cannot run unsupervised. Super-fast algorithms require super-fast safety systems that can keep up with the algorithms and detect when they are going off course, in which case they can either shut them down or make them safe. That is the painful lesson not just from Knight Capital but from the many other market crises we have witnessed. And, it is a lesson we must apply to the entire Internet of Things, as our lives become increasingly dependent on it.

A Personal Shopping Assistant that Knows You Better than You Do

Who wouldn't like to have a personal shopping assistant? Imagine an assistant that knows your tastes intimately, understanding that you will not consider any labels that are not from one of your favored designers. This dream shopping assistant is also aware of your spending habits and knows that you rarely pay full price for your designer gear, preferring special offers.

Your dream shopper also knows that you don't have the patience for Internet orders; instead, you like to seize an in-store bargain from one of your favorite boutiques, and you are a workaholic, so you shop only during your lunch break or on your way home. Who can afford such an assistant? Now, suppose that your assistant is not a human but, rather, a smart algorithm. The algorithm knows your spending habits, your current location and which products are available in stores—including price comparisons and special offers. Further, it can push relevant offers to you through your smart phone.

That is exactly the approach that forward-looking firms like DBS Bank in Singapore are pioneering. DBS calls this personal assistant a "Digital Concierge." DBS collaborates with retail partners to make highly personalized location-aware offers that enrich the lives of their customers, generate greater revenues for the retailers and enhance customer loyalty for the bank.

The Digital Concierge is an example of what is to come. We are at the cusp of a smart algorithm revolution that is fed by data coming from the Internet of Things and offers the potential to enrich your life wherever you go.

What if your favorite pizzeria could determine that you were driving by on your way home? It could pop your usual pizza into the oven and text you that it will be ready in 10 minutes. All you have to do is stop and pick it up. And, if you don't want it, the pizzeria can offer it in slices to other passersby—a win-win situation.

Or, perhaps you are in the market for a new laptop, and you go to a shopping mall to buy one using your bank credit card. You decide to shop later for a new laptop case. Meanwhile, your credit card has communicated your purchase and your possible need for a case to local retailers, one of which offers you a 30 percent discount. You duck in to take advantage of the discount and then receive a text message with another offer—this time for a 10 percent discount at a restaurant if you arrive within 30 minutes.

The idea of on-time offers is capturing the imagination of retailers large and small. With good reason: Turkcell, the leading Turkish mobile phone operator, has determined that customers are 10 times more likely to respond to on-time offers than to more generalized offers.

As more and more devices interact, individuals develop a richer digital identity. The more information that becomes accessible to service providers, the better they can understand their customers' needs and wants. Going further, this enhanced understanding gives them an even greater opportunity—to anticipate customers' every desire. Online retailer Amazon, an early adopter and innovative user of Big Data, went so far as to speculate that it might start delivering products before its customers order them.

Thingalytics

You may wonder what GE's power-generation engines, Knight Capital's "Knightmare on Wall Street" and DBS Bank's Digital Concierge have in common. On the surface, a smart power-generation engine looks nothing like a trading system run amok, which looks nothing like a smart marketing system. The truth is that all of these cases are all about Things.

Things are digitized objects, each with its own digital ID. They can be anything from a person, to a heart rate monitor, to a power-generation engine, to a vehicle, to a stock. All of these Things create data, and that data is often fast and big: "fast data," because it is often changing rapidly and streaming at us; "Big Data," because volumes quickly add up and because incoming data may also need to be cross-referenced and enriched by searching massive Big Data repositories.

Nearly everyone and everything can have a digital ID. In addition, a Thing communicates other data parameters in update "events" over the Internet as Things change. The GPS locator on your mobile device creates a data set that informs other people where you are. It also can remember where you have been and anticipate where you are going.

Thingalytics is about apps that drive smarter behavior and ultimately turn the Internet of Things into an intelligent, self-learning environment. To accomplish these goals, Thingalytics apps have to piece together the story of the Things, analyze the situation and make smart decisions. This situation is complicated by fast Big Data. Apps frequently face the challenge of searching for a needle in a haystack when the haystacks are moving past on a conveyer belt!

My term "Thingalytics" is a composite of "Things" and "Analytics." Analytics is the brains of an app; it

> **Thingalytics is about apps that drive smarter behavior and ultimately turn the Internet of Things into an intelligent, self-learning environment.**

performs the smart analysis to determine whether we should take an action. Analytics for Things has to be able cope with the scale, speed and complexity of the Internet of Things!

The Benefits of Thingalytics

Lessons learned from GE, Knight Capital and DBS allow us to immediately identify four benefits that we can gain by employing Thingalytics correctly:

> **> Thingalytics Benefit #1: Optimizing operations to increase efficiency**

As in GE's case, monitoring how a machine, a system or a business is running—plus monitoring the surrounding environmental conditions and making smart adjustments—can save us money, resources and time.

For example, we can:

- Match the nearest, most relevant doctor to a health crisis in a hospital
- Modify the course and speed of container ships, trucks or trains to reduce fuel usage
- Adjust the temperature in an office in response to the presence of people

In these and countless other ways a business can become smarter and more efficient by continuously optimizing Things.

To increase efficiency, one connected machine can help other machines by sensing and communicating information about its environment. As an example, an 18-wheel truck with sensors in its engine can send signals to other trucks in its convoy—informing the other engines about the gradients it encounters or inclement weather conditions, thereby helping the other trucks maximize fuel and brake performance.

One very hopeful side-effect of increased efficiency is the potential to improve health throughout the world; for example, medical professionals can treat more cases or prioritize the urgent cases. Further, we could reduce carbon emissions with fewer vehicles traveling along more efficient routes, combined with more efficient energy production.

> Thingalytics Benefit #2: Avoiding threats

Knight Capital is an example of how modern-day crises can come upon us faster than ever. Across all businesses, identifying and preventing impending risks, fraud and other threats before they become critical is vital to minimizing fines, losses and reputational damage. How firms detect, preempt and deal with these continuous disruptions, and whether they can transform them into opportunities, helps to define their competitive advantage. If, for example, monitors could have detected the early signs that Knight's algorithm was malfunctioning, such as too many orders and order pricing errors, they could have shut off its access to the market.

> Thingalytics Benefit #3: Seizing opportunities to increase revenue

Identifying "in-the-moment" opportunities to place an algorithmic trade, up-sell to a customer or push a smart offer (as per DBS Bank) all constitute new opportunities to increase revenue. Battles for business supremacy are already being fought based on first-mover advantage, where the Thingalytics algorithm that spots the opportunity first and moves on it is the winner.

> **Thingalytics Benefit # 4: Supercharging customer experience**

Radically improved predictive models of what individual customers do and do not want, driven by Big Data analytics, are revolutionizing consumer marketing. Combined with the opportunity for real-time location and context-aware applications, we can now push the right content in the right place at the right time. The result: happier customers.

Equally important is the capability to spot and deal with unhappy customers as early as possible. For example, if a hotel can identify a Diamond-tier guest who has been waiting to check in for 10 minutes, then the manager can head off his or her unhappiness by offering a "fast track" check in. This type of special treatment will not just solve the problem—it will also make the guest feel welcome. Or, consider a customer using an ATM machine that has run out of cash. A bank can proactively text a message of apology to the customer, along with a map to the nearest functioning ATM. Any organization that identifies issues proactively and responds sensitively engenders a warm response from its customers.

We'll see many examples of these four benefits as we explore real-world scenarios throughout this book.

Listening to Your Things

There is a certain Seussian ring to Thingalytics. It brings to mind Dr. Seuss's children's book *The Cat in the Hat*[6], where Thing 1 and Thing 2 were both troublemakers and problem solvers. Thing 1 and Thing 2 were known for their ability to find anything—"anything, anything under the sun!"

Thingalytics is the opposite: Keeping track of Things is difficult, and extracting insights from the constantly streaming updates is even more difficult. At the same time, Thingalytics becomes immensely valuable

---

6 http://en.wikipedia.org/wiki/The_Cat_in_the_Hat

after you have devised the killer apps. A key lesson we shall see throughout this book is that discovering those apps involves a process of experimentation. It all starts with tapping into the fast Big Data flowing from the Things. Collecting Big Data and not analyzing it is like collecting stamps and not showing them to anyone. Innovative firms don't know for certain if their theories are right; they start experimenting, measure the results and adapt quickly.

> **A key lesson we shall see throughout this book is that discovering killer apps involves a process of experimentation.**

If patterns in the data about Things that tell a story can be identified and utilized properly, then they can provide companies with exciting and profitable opportunities. If not, they can sit unnoticed and unloved at the bottom of dark, dank databases. You have to put the Big Data about Things to work; otherwise, it is useless. You need to find insights and act upon them quickly, because you frequently have only a short time window to respond.

> **If patterns in the data about Things that tell a story can be identified and utilized properly, then they can provide companies with exciting and profitable opportunities.**

Big Data and the Things of the Internet are the fuel with which a new generation of companies will power their profits. McKinsey[7] Global Institute identifies Big Data the next frontier for innovation, competition

---

[7] McKinsey & Company, McKinsey Global Institute, June, 2010: "Big data: The next frontier for innovation, competition, and productivity." http://www.mckinsey.com/insights/business_technology/big_data_the_next_frontier_for_innovation

and productivity. The amounts of data being created are so voluminous that they are measured in quintillions (10^{18}) of bytes: 2.5 quintillion bytes of new data are created every day. Every byte created adds to the innumerable bytes that already exist—and they can tell us a story. The story might be about the personal spending habits of an iPhone user, or it could be about the engine capabilities of an 18-wheel truck, or an overspending trading platform. The trick is to winkle out the story, thus identifying a trend, a pattern or an anomaly that you can use.

Enterprise Empowerment

The Internet of Things is causing a great deal of excitement among many corporations, which believe that Big Data will drive future profits. McKinsey claims, for example, that a retailer using Big Data to its full capacity "could increase its operating margin by more than 60 percent."

Similarly, Gartner describes Big Data and the Internet of Things as the beginning of a new era, the "Digital Industrial Economy." Peter Sondergaard, Senior Vice President at Gartner[8] and global head of research, offered the following perspective on the new digital world: "Every budget is an IT budget, every company is a technology company, every business is becoming a digital leader and every person is becoming a technology company."

> **"The digital winners are ruthlessly and fearlessly creating the digital industrial economy."**
> **Dave Aron, Gartner**

Gartner Fellow Dave Aron explains: "The digital winners are ruthlessly and fearlessly creating the digital industrial economy. Roles are changing. Business models are changing. Timeframes are changing. Industry and company boundaries are blurring. We can't rely on old practices, safe relationships, legacy

---

8 Marketwatch, October 7, 2013: "Gartner Says It's the Beginning of a New Era: The Digital Industrial Economy."

technologies and known vendors. We have to explore, adapt and adopt new digital realities. We have to be fearless digital leaders."

Thingalytics is the future for fearless digital leaders who don't want to fly blind. The digital world is there for the taking; the sky is the limit. If we do not use it, however, we risk being left behind and called digitally myopic.

Exploring Thingalytics the Book

In this book we will explore many real-world examples of Thingalytics in action, and we will meet several visionaries who are involved in pioneering these new apps. We will analyze the lessons learned by these innovators, and we will explore what the future can bring. We will also consider what the technology implications are and how we can cope with them.

In Chapter 1, "It's All About Me," we explore how Thingalytics is empowering a new generation of personalized marketing and customer experience applications.

In Chapter 2, "Machines with Feelings," we look into industrial and retail processes and consider how smarter machines are enhancing efficiency, reducing costs and improving customer experience.

In Chapter 3, "Home Is Where the Smart Is," we investigate how new intelligent Thingalytics apps are revolutionizing cooking, cleaning, washing and TV watching.

In Chapter 4, "Take Two Smart Pills and Call Me in the Morning," we examine the hospital of the future and how it is already manifesting itself today.

In Chapter 5, "I'm the Chairman of the Board," we explore smart self-learning algorithms that function as the "brains" of Thingalytics, focusing particularly on automated trading.

In Chapter 6, "RoboCops: Smarter than the Average Criminal," we delve into how we can spot and ideally navigate around threats and problems, including some thoughts as to how Knight Capital and similar crises could have been avoided.

In Chapter 7, "Planes, Trains and Automobiles," we discuss Thingalytics apps for smart logistics and autonomous transport systems.

In Chapter 8, "The Technology Behind Thingalytics," we explore some of the technology issues involved in supporting massive-scale Thingalytics apps, and we consider how new Big Data streaming analytics architectures in the cloud could be the key to successfully meeting this challenge.

Finally, Chapter 9, "Go Forth and Use Thingalytics!" concludes our discussion by summarizing the lessons learned and explaining how you can move forward and use Thingalytics to improve your business.

Happy reading!

1

It's All About Me

Ozlem's Shoes

Ozlem Demirboga has barely enough time to grab a sandwich at lunch-time, never mind shopping for the designer shoes that she loves. Today, however, as she leaves her office in Istanbul, Turkey, to pick up some lunch, she receives a text message on her mobile phone that is too good to pass up.

What is this special message? It is an announcement from a boutique on the next street for a promotion for 20 percent off top designer shoes if she comes in within the next hour. Ozlem[9] has time to take a quick detour, and she picks up a great pair of discounted shoes.

It is no coincidence that Ozlem loves designer shoes and that she received a promotion for them. Ozlem is not just an ordinary mobile user. She happens to be in charge of customer experience management at Turkish mobile carrier Turkcell. In fact, she was responsible for the mobile location-aware promotion application that just sent her the message. The message came from a new breed of real-time marketing systems that can make informed and relevant offers in exactly the right place and at exactly the right time to exactly the right customer.

Turkcell has a huge customer base with more than 34 million mobile subscribers. It also has an incredible opportunity to innovate with cutting-edge services that can increase revenues. To achieve these goals, however, Ozlem must make these services attractive and "sticky"—a positive experience that discourages subscribers from going over to other carriers.

Ozlem and her team have launched a series of smart applications designed around the mobile user, which are winning Turkcell new customers and increasing the average revenue per user (ARPU). These smart applications are location- and context-aware. In other words, they track the locations and behaviors of customers who have "opted in," meaning

---

[9] Ozlem has since left Turkcell in order to pursue a graduate degree.

they have shared their preferences, likes and dislikes. By enabling marketers to carefully target appropriate customers, these applications can dynamically improve the experiences of those customers.

The criteria of right place, right time and relevance are all important to a successful mobile promotion. Getting even one of these criteria wrong can seriously annoy a customer.

I Want It All; I Want It Now

About 25 years ago, the Internet was extremely disruptive to traditional "bricks-and-mortar" retail businesses. New online retailers such as Amazon took market share away from "Main Street" by offering a greater choice of merchandise, immediate availability and speedy delivery. This was shopping in a new, virtual world.

The Internet of Things is poised to completely disrupt that model. In today's mobile era consumers are increasingly using smart phones equipped with location-tracking sensors. The unfolding wearable computing era is adding smart watches and, soon, smart "heads-up-display" glasses—integrating information on-the-go into our interactions in the real world. This means that, using Thingalytics, we can start to overlay information about the real world around us in a real-time, location- and context-aware manner.

Using Thingalytics, we can start to overlay information about the real world around us in a real-time, location- and context-aware manner.

All of this mobile technology, from cell phones to tablets and wearable devices, affords us instant gratification. Because we have this technology at our fingertips, we are becoming increasingly demanding. Today waiting even 24 hours to order an item online is too long! We want it all, we want it now and we don't want to spend a lot of time searching for it. Thus, location-awareness, combined with a hunger for real-time, is creating something new! We want the digital world to read our mind and plot a course to our heart's desire. This doesn't mean, however, that we're prepared to receive irrelevant solicitations. Just the opposite: We are growing ever more impatient in our expectations that our online experience be completely personalized.

As a result, mobile technology, combined with Thingalytics, has fueled a new wave of applications that embrace this impatience. These apps are designed to enhance the next generation of customer experience to make customers feel special by seeking out their interests and enriching their experiences in the "real world." And yes, Main Street can use Thingalytics to fight back!

> We want the digital world to read our mind and plot a course to our heart's desire.

Mobile devices and applications create a wellspring of fast Big Data that in turn helps firms to refine and enhance their offerings for mobile users—if they use this data properly! This new generation of applications empowers retailers, telecommunications providers, banks, hotels and other companies to tailor a user's every experience. By explicitly embracing the opportunities created by mobility—including tracking/location—and by personalizing the customers' experience, a business can make customers feel that they are receiving special treatment.

Main Street can use Thingalytics to tap into the mobile, location-aware world, which offers tremendous opportunities to reduce costs and increase revenues. Thanks to GPS and other location tracking, your mobile device knows where you are at any given time. Today's technology enables service providers to filter the world for you—and only you. Personalization is the future of mobility: In the end, it is all about me. And I want it now!

Right Place, Right Time, Not Spam

Receiving a promotion for something that is too far away to be convenient, or receiving it too late—after you've left the area or after the offer has expired—is very frustrating. Most importantly, however, receiving a promotion for something that is not relevant to you is just like being subjected to spam email. You might overlook this type of message once or twice, but receiving spam frequently is extremely annoying. Further, receiving it on your mobile phone feels like a breach of privacy: It is following you on your personal device! You could rapidly become fed up with your mobile carrier and perhaps even change networks.

Customers changing networks is a mobile carrier's worst nightmare. The technical term used by mobile carriers for subscribers who leave is "churn."

> **Customers changing networks is a mobile carrier's worst nightmare.**

Customer churn and retention levels have long plagued providers. Many studies have estimated that churn rates range between 20 percent and 30 percent in most regions.

Mobile carriers focus on three primary objectives:

1. **Increasing market share**
   - Carriers can attract new customers by launching new, innovative services before their competitors do, or by simply offering a better quality of service than the competition.

2. **Maximizing the average revenue per user (ARPU)**
   - Making as much money as possible from customers by maximizing the purchasing potential of each and every subscriber.

3. Minimizing churn

- Making services "sticky" so customers don't change networks. This is a key goal, because winning new customers is many times more expensive than retaining existing ones.

A mobile promotions application addresses all three concerns:

1. It attracts new customers by offering an innovative service that personalizes their experiences and makes compelling offers that are directly targeted to them.

2. It has the potential to attract new subscribers and increase ARPU, provided it doesn't spam them.

3. It minimizes churn, if it is implemented properly. If not, then it can be perceived as spam and consequently can increase churn.

As Ozlem walks down the streets of Istanbul, thousands of other workers and shoppers are also going about their business. Significantly, almost all of them are carrying cell phones. The majority of them subscribe to the same mobile carrier as Ozlem—Turkcell. However, only Ozlem and a few other subscribers will receive the promotion about the designer shoes. Specifically, only those customers whom the retailer has identified as nearby, interested and highly relevant will receive the promotion. Thousands of other subscribers who are nearby will not receive this offer. Several of them, however, will receive different offers that are more relevant to their interests as well as their spending and shopping habits.

It is not just complex applications like location-aware promotions that can yield results. Ozlem cites the example of an enhancement to an existing simple application that proved highly successful. The application was designed to "up-sell," or to convince prepaid Turkcell subscribers to purchase additional minutes. Many subscribers prepay, buying minutes on a pay-as-you-go basis. Turkcell developed an application that monitors subscribers' remaining minutes. If they are likely to run out of minutes during a call, then the application sends them an offer to purchase additional time there and then.

Ozlem contends that sending the message to customers before they run out of minutes has made the application many times more profitable than the previous version, which delivered a message only after the minutes had run out. The previous version relied on offline, batch-based analysis of remaining minutes. The new version utilizes a real-time event-driven approach to proactively send out an offer before the prepaid minutes expire.

> **Whether it is a simple application or a highly complex one, the winning characteristics are the same: right place, right time, not spam.**

Whether it is a simple application or a highly complex one, the winning characteristics are the same: right place, right time, not spam. Achieving these characteristics requires continuous and proactive monitoring, analysis and response to huge amounts of ever-changing events.

Location, Location, Location

Mobile applications that respond to the changing locations of people or things are becoming more commonplace. Location tracking can be applied to animals on a farm, vehicles in a supply chain, cars on highways, packages in a distribution network and pallets in a warehouse. Tracking these people, animals and things can feed data into bespoke applications that deliver the customer experience. And, this is just the beginning. Location-aware applications are going to feature prominently in responsive 21st century businesses, for two primary reasons:

1. The applications are increasingly easy to build and deploy.

2. The location-tracking hardware and mobile devices that control the applications are widely available.

The tracking technology in Turkcell's location-aware promotions application triangulates the location of the cell phone ID that is built into the wireless handset. Unlike some GPS-based applications, this approach can work inside office buildings and shopping malls—a real benefit for Turkcell's promotions.

Using Thingalytics, Turkcell can process and make smart decisions on the huge data flows coming in from their 35 million mobile subscribers. The data includes location changes, user preference and/or behavior updates, information about new location-aware campaigns being launched, and changes to existing campaigns. Thingalytics helps to make Turkcell all about the customer.

Disruptive Disintermediation, Dynamic Offers

Disintermediation—the practice of removing the middleman—has haunted banks for many years. It began with customers investing their money in the stock market, rather than with their local bank, supplanting agents, brokers and resellers in the process. Today, thanks to the Internet, applications such as PayPal and Google Wallet are all contributing to bank disintermediation. The creation of the "mobile wallet"—with the ability to organize, store and access everything in your wallet from your mobile phone—has opened up the world of mobile payments and is giving traditional banks a scare.

> **Thanks to the Internet, applications such as PayPal and Google Wallet are all contributing to bank disintermediation.**

Banks surveyed in a 2013 study[10], when mobile wallets had yet to take off, identified companies such as Google as the biggest threat to their business due to these companies' mobile wallet offerings. Today, businesses from PayPal to Google to Starbucks are offering customized versions of their mobile wallets, along with discounts, promotions and loyalty schemes that make their products stickier. They are also creating a sticky situation for traditional banks that are mired in the old-fashioned checking account and credit card business model.

Not surprisingly, many banks have developed creative new strategies to counteract this threat. For example, DBS, Singapore's largest bank and one of the leading regional banks in Asia, came up with an idea to beat the disintermediating mobile wallet disruptors at their own game. The bank launched some revolutionary mobile services for its customers that have increased both customer loyalty and the utilization of DBS's financial products.

David Backley, the Managing Director for Consumer Bank Technology at DBS, concedes that one of the basic drivers for developing these new services was the threat of the mobile wallet. David and DBS implemented a strategy to take the bank's game to the next level by adopting a leadership position in "mobile, intelligent banking."

The first step was to get closer to customers and provide them with a better credit card experience, to encourage them to pay using their cards rather than a mobile wallet application. As David explained: "Ideally we'd like to have a personal relationship manager for every customer; someone who knows each customer and personalizes his or her banking experience. But it's impossible to have human relationship managers for 4 million people. So, we decided to use technology as the relationship manager."

---

[10] Elliott Holley, Banking Technology, October 21, 2013: "Google is banks' biggest fear finds innovation survey." http://www.bankingtech.com/177022/google-is-banks-biggest-fear-finds-innovation-survey/

In Singapore people frequently shop and eat out. They usually take their credit cards and mobile phones with them. They also like to receive special offers. David wanted to make these offers in real-time, based on customer location, interests and characteristics, rather than after-the-fact.

> "We decided to use technology as the relationship manager."
> David Backley, DBS

To create real-time, mobile phone-delivered services, DBS needed the capability to analyze and respond intelligently to events as they unfolded. In other words, the special offers had to reach the customers while they were close to their shopping and dining facilities.

"We're in a unique position—where all of our interactions with customers happen in real-time," David explains. "You need event-driven analytics to decide what you do with such interactions or events."

DBS customers can (of course) access their accounts on mobile devices. They can also opt in to receive carefully targeted and relevant cross-sell and up-sell offers both while they are shopping and after they have purchased items with their credit cards.

Consider this scenario: You go into a computer store to buy a new laptop. You select the laptop, but you don't buy a laptop bag because you want to shop around first. Your propensity to shop around for the bag is not as unique as you might think. In fact, a computer model predicted that you were going to do just that.

How could a computer "know" this? The answer is that it found that nearly 75 percent of people of your gender, age range, socioeconomic class and spending habits are likely to do the same thing. Of course, the store where you purchased your laptop wants to sell you the laptop bag. So, it sends you a text message offer for 25 percent off any laptop bag if you complete the purchase within the next 15 minutes. The store, in partnership with the bank, has made this promotion. They really want your business.

This kind of responsive cross-sell and up-sell application opens up a whole new world of possibilities. Although targeting you through your mobile device is the ultimate goal, the bank can still offer you deals without one. For example, when you swipe your credit card, DBS knows where you are, and it can make an offer to you via the store. However, the really compelling opportunity is to provide services in the same style as Turkcell. For customers who opt in, the bank can push opportunities based on right place, right time and relevant offers to customers' smart phones.

Because a bank collects a great deal of financial information about its customers, it is in a powerful position to categorize customers and statistically predict the behavior of people in certain categories. The bank can analyze your likelihood to purchase a particular product based on your previous buying habits and which "buckets" the statistical computer models put you in. For example, it can determine whether you are more likely to buy a product in a store or over the web. You would then receive the promotional offers wherever you shop. The bank's partners want to target the most relevant customers—and the bank has a good shot at it by using Thingalytics.

Time to Eat

Dynamic offers are not limited to stores; they can also be used for many other retail offerings including travel, hotels and even food. Consider a customer in the young executive salary bracket who is looking to purchase an expensive camera or DVD player at a shopping mall with her DBS credit card. Within minutes she will get a discount offer for a popular nearby restaurant. The restaurant is making an offer—through the bank—of a certain discount for a small window of time. When the customer pays the restaurant bill, again with her bank's card, she may receive an SMS offer for a prize draw that encourages her to continue shopping at the mall.

Of course the bank knows your credit worthiness as well, so it can up-sell to you in another way. When a customer makes a large purchase such as a flat-screen TV using a DBS credit card, the bank can analyze the customer's credit score and, if appropriate, initiate a call from customer care to offer an installment plan. Paying off the purchase in, say, 12 monthly installments benefits both the consumer and the bank—which makes a profit and ensures that the customer still has available credit on his or her card for future purchases. Similarly, if a customer uses a DBS credit card to pay for travel services such as a flight, the bank or a partner can try to up-sell a relevant travel insurance policy just as the customer is booking the trip.

David of DBS maintains that as the bank learns more about the science behind real-time campaigns, it can fine-tune these efforts. For example, it could tweak offers throughout the day to enhance their effectiveness, based on continuous analysis of the campaign's performance. The ongoing visibility of campaign efficacy is enabled by real-time dashboards, which provide the credit card team with continuous insight. It is possible to monitor the parameters of a campaign based on key performance indicators (KPIs) to ascertain whether the campaign has achieved the predicted number of responses within a time window. Firms can also determine whether a limited availability offer is in danger of being oversubscribed. If it is, then they could remove the offer and replace it with a similar one to avoid disappointing customers.

> **The ongoing visibility of campaign efficacy is enabled by real-time dashboards, which provide the credit card team with continuous insight.**

Of course, services that have so much visibility into customers' information raise many privacy concerns. To address these concerns, David emphasizes that it is critical that such services are opt in and that customers have tight control over the contact policy. For example, a customer may indicate that he or she wants no more than one marketing message per day. The system must honor this request or risk damaging the bank's relationship with the customer.

> **For example, a customer may indicate that he or she wants no more than one marketing message per day.**

Intelligent Pricing

Building on the thinking behind DBS's dynamic offering services, one compelling scenario I see in the future is intelligent pricing. Imagine if there were no fixed prices for products. Instead, a smart pricing system could adjust the price up or down depending on demand and/or other parameters.

> **Imagine if there were no fixed prices for products.**

This scenario is similar to the advanced pricing models used at banks' dealing desks for over-the-counter bond and currency markets. The banks respond to electronic requests for quotes (RFQs) by categorizing customers into bands and then adjusting the spread; that is, the amount of profit the banks receive from each transaction. The spread depends on how attractive the bank finds the customer's business and how likely the customer is to accept the bank's quote.

It is interesting to think about such advanced real-time pricing models finding their way into the consumer realm. Banks such as DBS and credit card companies, in conjunction with retail partners, are well placed to offer such services.

Smart Theme Parks

A great example of Thingalytics being used in a smart environment is a visionary project being developed at Disney Parks called "Next Generation Experience" (NGE). In a February 2011 article in the Orlando Sentinel, Disney's Parks and Resorts Chairman Tom Staggs revealed some of the park's $1 billion project. Spurred by guests' complaints about long wait times for rides and other popular attractions, Disney Parks developed NGE as "a version of Fast Pass for an entire Disney vacation." Future guests will be able to provide their preferences and even pre-book rides, attractions and seats at shows and restaurants before leaving home.

The more compelling opportunity, however, is the real-time, dynamic personalization of the Disney experience. Once guests arrive, the park will be able to determine who they are and where they are—and then personalize their experience. The tracking technology is likely to consist of radio frequency identification, or RFID, tags embedded in wristbands. Another option involves smart apps downloaded to location-enabled smart phones. A smart app would provide navigation assistance around the park and would also be able to make recommendations based on individual customer preferences. For example, if your ride of choice has very long lines, then the NGE app could recommend an alternative ride and even book you a slot. Anyone who has had to wait for an hour or more with small children to get into "It's a Small World" in 95-degree heat can appreciate the value of this technology.

> Being able to track the locations of guests and even re-route them dynamically enables the parks to make optimal use of their resources.

Going further, if the park knows your location, then it can also optimize the movements of the "cast," the Disney characters such as Snow White and Goofy that wander around the park. Cast members can seek out particular guests because they know where they are. Another bonus when small children are becoming fractious in the heat!

From Disney's point of view, the NGE project offers outstanding business benefits. Being able to track the locations of guests and even re-route them dynamically enables the parks to make optimal use of their resources.

Pursuing this line of thought, Disney can take the same approach as Turkcell by offering mobile, targeted, location-aware promotions. For example, it can highlight special offers on photos taken on rides or on merchandise that fits the guests' interests and spending habits as the guests move around the park. By applying these principles Disney can radically increase the average value per guest. Guests will have much more time to spend money if they are not spending the bulk of their day waiting in line—plus they will be in a much better mood!

Gambling on Technology

I witnessed another effective strategy to improve the customer experience while also minimizing fraud when I was working with a large casino chain in the Asia-Pacific region. The chain operates a loyalty card system in which patrons earn points for playing different games in a casino. To earn these points patrons need to swipe their loyalty card at each gaming table. When patrons earn enough points they receive some type of reward; for example, a free dinner. Because customers have to swipe in at each game, the casino knows who is playing at each table. Further, because dealers have to enter wins and losses on a mini keyboard at the gaming tables, the casino also knows, both in real-time and over time, each player's win-loss profile.

And, the benefits to the casino can go even further. The technology tracks the movements of gaming chips through the casino by embedding them with RFID tags. This technology enables management to track the chips throughout the casino. This system helps to ensure there is no foul play—which benefits the majority of gamblers as well as the casino.

Utilizing all of this technology alongside Thingalytics has enabled the casino to implement an extremely advanced fraud surveillance system. For example, the casino can detect potential collusion among players or between players and dealers. Even though the casino employs only a handful of surveillance experts who know what to look for, it has thousands of surveillance cameras. When the casino detects potential fraud, it can automatically feed the output of the nearest camera to a surveillance expert who can make a judgment as to what is going on. There is an upside to this arrangement—the casino can respond intelligently when high rollers are in town and shower them with love and attention, thereby encouraging customer loyalty.

Smart Hotels

I have been involved in a very exciting Thingalytics project that is being run by a major global hotel chain. The chain wants to provide a better customer experience by being able to identify people who stay frequently, determine where they are in their hotels and evaluate the kind of experience they are having. To achieve this, they are using "inside" location-tracking technologies. Members of the loyalty scheme can download a smart app that can then track their experience in the hotel, giving them the ability to receive offers and giving the hotel the ability to continuously learn about customer behavior and respond when opportunities present themselves to enhance a customer's experience.

The hotel employs two main location-tracking technologies:

- iBeacon technology, which uses low-power Bluetooth to detect when a patron's cell phone is nearby.

- Technology from Aruba Networks, which uses Wi-Fi signal strength to determine in which zone a patron is located.

With these technologies, combined with Thingalytics, some compelling applications are being developed. One application is used by front desk staff. As patrons line up to check in, the staff can tell who is in the line, how long they have waited and their tier in the loyalty program. A Gold member waiting a long time might trigger extra staff being diverted to the check-in area or a visit from the manager.

> As patrons line up to check in, the staff can tell who is in the line, how long they have waited and their tier in the loyalty program.

Another application can track which zones of the hotel its patrons visit both on their first trip and on subsequent trips. They might notice, for example, that patrons tend not to visit a particular restaurant on their first trip. After they have eaten there, however, most patrons go back. This pattern suggests that the restaurant is not easy to find but it is popular once patrons discover it. So, perhaps the hotel should improve the signage! Building on this data, the hotel can track the sentiments conveyed by social media postings in particular areas. For example, a Tweet claiming "terrible meal" posted from within the restaurant probably means the hotel needs to look into quality control—and fast!

"Super" Markets

Another exciting project I have experienced introduces another sensory technology: video analytics. A major supermarket chain, which would prefer to remain incognito for now, is experimenting with a system that incorporates cameras and digital signage in multiple stores. Combined with Thingalytics, these technologies can track customers and personalize a shop—even without knowing who the customers are. In other words, customers do not even need to carry a smart phone! Cameras and digital signs located throughout the stores enable the supermarket to track everyone's shopping experience and to tempt shoppers to look for and take up offers they might otherwise have missed.

One particularly interesting video analytics algorithm can conduct facial analysis on every customer who walks past. It can determine whether customers are male or female, their approximate age and even how happy they are—by tracking their facial expressions!

Firms can use this technology to explore real-time demographic-driven marketing. For example, they can establish a metric such as: "If more than two men over 30 are standing in area X and at least one of them looks sad, then play this offer on the nearest screen." The offer might say "Cheer up—special offer on beer—two for the price of one. Come to Aisle Y and print a coupon." By tracking coupon use at checkout, the supermarket can calculate the take-up rate. They can then use this data to assess the effectiveness of the offer.

Ideally, specific offers are targeted at particular demographics, and they can be adjusted depending on the desired target audience. Stores can employ this visual analysis approach to Thingalytics to vary offers based on how people are feeling. It used to be that only people could judge you by your facial expressions. Now algorithms are doing it too!!

Conclusions

The next decade will be absolutely fascinating. Wearable computing is going to go mainstream. Google Glass is one device that particularly interests me. This is a wearable glass that can project information on a tiny screen. Actually, it isn't very good—but as this book goes to print Google is removing it from the market to focus on improvements[11]. In the next decade we are going to see more nonintrusive wearable glasses that can project information directly into your line of sight.

---

[11] http://techcrunch.com/2015/01/19/today-is-the-last-day-to-buy-google-glass/

So, as you walk down the street and look into a store window, items that interest you will be highlighted. As you approach the store, items will be priced personally for you—based on your propensity to buy and your membership in loyalty schemes. Comparison prices with other nearby stores might also be listed. When you gaze at a coffee shop sign, your display will identify all of your social media friends who are in there—so you can meet them for coffee (or avoid them)! When you look at a bus, your glasses indicate the route; that way you know it is the right bus. You can also see how close the nearest taxi cab is—because your Uber or Lyft app is integrated into your glasses.

This kind of augmented reality view will essentially mash up the entire cloud and personalize and localize it for you. These technologies will need to analyze billions of updates per second to determine whom a company's products or offers are relevant to, to provide this personalized view. The software architectures behind this kind of app require a new science of smart Big Data analytics, which we explore in Chapter 7.

The mobile, wearable revolution is simultaneously an opportunity for and a threat to businesses. For the banks, shops, telecommunications companies, casinos, hotels and supermarkets that seize the opportunity, Main Street is becoming Mobility Street, with a chance to assume a leadership position as their industry transforms.

As we walk around with our smart phones and sophisticated tablets, we create clouds of real-time, fast Big Data that Thingalytics-savvy users can "translate" into information to provide us with an enhanced customer experience. The banking, shopping, casino or hotel customer who is offered a personalized location-aware experience might spend more money, feel better and become more loyal. Right place, right time and relevant is the key. It has to be all about me!

> **The mobile, wearable revolution is simultaneously an opportunity for and a threat to businesses.**

For the retailer, hotelier, bank or telecommunications company the benefits of Thingalytics are also enormous. These entities can learn what their customers want and how they behave, to help improve their business. They can also spot immediately when their customers are most receptive to an offer. Equally as important, they can spot when something is going wrong; for example, an ATM machine runs out of cash or a customer is waiting in line for too long. Finally, they might be able to spot fraud more easily because algorithms can track errant behaviors faster than humans can.

We are fast approaching an augmented reality world, where wearable computing, combined with Thingalytics, beams the personal experience straight into our line of site. I am genuinely concerned about what some compulsive shopaholics might achieve with this personal shopping radar!

Machines with Feelings

The Meaning of Life

In Douglas Adam's *Hitchhiker's Guide to the Galaxy*[12] a computer called Deep Thought was asked to provide the answer to Life, the Universe and Everything. After the great computer program had run for "a very quick seven-and-a-half-million years," it answered: "42."

Although Deep Thought was fictional, the difficulty it encountered in solving a very human query shows us how challenging it can be to create truly artificially intelligent computers—machines that possess human traits such as self-learning. The possibilities of artificial intelligence (AI), such as driverless cars and robots that can "feel," continue to fascinate. In fact, technology mavens including Google, Facebook and Microsoft are buying AI companies[13] and advancing their nuanced visions of machines with feelings.

To date, however, the quest for machines that possess the characteristics of a human brain remains in its infancy. Today's machines are like an "exploded body" where the body parts transmit signals to a remote brain to analyze. Sensors constitute the nerve endings in these body parts, sending signals to the brain, which is in reality a computer. This brain is where Thingalytics takes place, to respond to the sensory feelings and generate a smart response, which could adjust parts of the body to optimize performance and take advantage of the current environment.

> **The quest for machines that possess the characteristics of a human brain remains in its infancy.**

For example, a company with 1,000 smart wind turbines—each equipped with networked sensors—can send information to a computer at headquarters—the brain—which will analyze performance and current

---

[12] http://en.wikipedia.org/wiki/The_Hitchhiker%27s_Guide_to_the_Galaxy
[13] http://www.forbes.com/sites/centurylink/2014/06/30/how-artificial-intelligence-could-change-your-business/

power requirements and adjust the behavior of individual turbines accordingly. Sensors can also supply the brain with continuous information to keep track of how many hours their sensitive internal mechanisms have been working. If these hours are excessive, then the brain can trigger an alert and schedule a maintenance call.

> **The goal of Thingalytics is to digitize information, analyze it and then make smart decisions based on the analysis.**

The goal of Thingalytics is to digitize information, analyze it and then make smart decisions based on the analysis. Although existing technology can perform these tasks, and can do so much faster than humans, the challenge lies with adding the human qualities that transcend automated responses.

By equipping machines with senses—particularly sight, sound and touch—modern technology can go a long way toward replicating some human qualities. In Thailand, for example, a government-financed committee has invented a robot that can taste Thai food and then determine whether it is authentic[14]. The robot, called e-Delicious, contains sensors and computer circuitry that act as an "electronic tongue and nose." e-Delicious contains nine sensors to determine the balance of six Thai flavors—sweet, sour, bitter, salty, savory and spicy—as well as the aroma. I wonder if e-Delicious can ask for water if the chef has made the curry too hot!

Current science is not the only medium that is considering the marriage of machines with human emotions. Science fiction can also help us to understand where we might go in the future. For example, in *Star Trek: The Next Generation*, Lieutenant Commander Data[15] was an android designed to self-learn the qualities and mannerisms of humans so that

---

[14] Jonathan Head, BBC News, November 25, 2014: "Thai Tasting Robot Tastes for Authenticity." http://www.bbc.com/news/world-asia-30110282
[15] http://www.startrek.com/database_article/data

he could become more human-like himself. Nevertheless, he remained a machine, even when he was equipped with an "emotion chip" to help him better understand human behaviors.

Right now, state-of-the-art technologies employ Thingalytics to optimize processes in complex industrial and domestic environments, by enabling them with sensors and then processing their sensory input. And there is *a lot* of input. Consider, for example, that an Airbus A380 produces more Big Data on a run from Frankfurt to Sydney than is housed in the entire Library of Congress in Washington, D.C.!

Like Commander Data's emotion chip, sensors can be added to existing systems to augment them with feelings ranging from the pain of failing components to the joy of running smoothly. We then utilize these feelings to optimize the ways the business works, specifically: doing more with less, saving money through reduced fuel usage, reducing waste and optimizing performance. In this chapter we explore how visionaries are already achieving these goals.

Things Go Better with Coke

A large cooler full of Coca-Cola products hums away quietly in the back of the convenience store. The cooler may not appear to doing much of anything apart from ensuring that customers have a plentiful supply of icy Diet Coke on hand. But in reality it is doing a lot more than that. If you look a little closer you might see a sticker, about the size of four quarters stuck together, on the Coca-Cola cooler.

This sticker, dubbed "Red Tag" by its creators, is actually a Low Energy Bluetooth-enabled device that can sense temperature, vibration, the proximity of other coolers, motion and its own location. Red Tag is what gives the Coca-Cola cooler *feelings*—sight, sound and touch—along with the ability to communicate these feelings. Coca-Cola can use this technology to automatically inventory their in-store equipment using any smart phone.

Red Tag is the brainchild of Kevin Flowers, Chief Technology Officer of Coca-Cola Enterprises (CCE). Kevin's team created Red Tag, also called a "beacon," to inventory its assets in the field. Prior to Red Tag, a salesperson had to visit the customer's store, write down the serial numbers of the coolers for inventory purposes and then physically take them back to the office. Now, the Red Tag Bluetooth solution is integrated into the salesperson's cell phone application. He or she can hit "Scan" and obtain an instant inventory of which coolers are present within the store. This is used for account management purposes and automatically updates CCE's customer relationship management (CRM) system.

A Low Energy Bluetooth-enabled device gives the Coca-Cola cooler *feelings* — sight, sound and touch — along with the ability to communicate these feelings.

Kevin concedes there were some challenges with implementing Red Tag. For example, the initial Bluetooth battery prototype had less than a year's life expectancy. "We innovated through that, and now we have nine-year battery life which brings the return on investment to a viable opportunity level," Kevin explains.

Red Tag will be the cornerstone of Coca-Cola Enterprises' Internet of Things strategy. "The core of our digital strategy is integration, which is a key enabler to agility in companies. If you can make data easily accessible, it opens up a whole new world where you can pursue emerging digital capabilities. Red Tag is the first step in this process. This opened up whole new world of leveraging mobile communications, enabling the assets in new ways beyond our initial concepts." Going further, Kevin recognized that Red Tag could move beyond Coke's field operations and be useful in customer engagement: "In the future we can create applications that interact with customers and shoppers."

When Kevin tested a prototype Red Tag, it was an instant success. In fact, Coca-Cola's business leaders were so impressed that they requested over 250,000 Red Tags. Kevin recounts: "That capability is the sum of all of the tablets, PCs and smart phones we have ever deployed. Suddenly you can have almost 250,000 Red Tags that add fast data, real data, and smart data to your enterprise operations. Now we have got a Big Data opportunity."

Kevin contends that Red Tag is in reality a next-generation platform whose true value has yet to be revealed. "The approach was that by making the information easily accessible, it was easier to pursue digital capabilities. This is a key differentiator for us."

The first use-case, taking inventory of coolers, was a simple one. However, Kevin wanted to push the envelope further by integrating the same capability into Coca-Cola's manufacturing environment. So, he installed Red Tags in one of the company's largest plants, located in Wakefield, England. Coca-Cola now boasts a completely sensor-enabled manufacturing environment, where it can begin to discover ways to make its processes smarter. This is critical in an operation that relies on hundreds of motors that can overheat or break down and several kilometers of conveyors that can break down and interrupt the entire production line.

The ease with which Coca-Cola can now connect to its assets, factories and trucks is key. Kevin explains: "We can connect within a couple of days. We can monitor temperature, vibration, proximity—and it does not have to be something traditionally wired. We just use the Red Tags."

Connectivity enabled Coca-Cola to transition from not knowing what was happening with their products to knowing a lot more. The company can then utilize this knowledge to examine trends and perform some fast data analytics. From there it can predict when something is going to happen. "It is all about confidence and trust," Kevin states. "If we see something repeated often enough, we can have confidence that it is going to happen again."

Connectivity opens up a world of visibility, right down to the most granular level. "We can see what is really happening in our business."

Of course, the more connections a company has, the more data it will receive. Kevin says: "There is so much information, that it requires large data analytics to make use of it. We have to figure out ways to filter through the real things we need to know."

Hockey Sticks and IoT

Looking at a graph of Internet of Things (IoT) adoption is like looking at a hockey stick: The graph slopes suddenly and sharply upward and then continues to rise much more gradually. The sharp angle of the graph is where PCs, smart phones and tablets came into play, according to Kevin. "It shows where we have been over history and where we are going in the next years. The opportunity now is the sum of all these prior generations, but when will that be real?"

Kevin is convinced that we are on the verge of witnessing some exciting innovations using IoT. Meantime: "The IoT is not always about buying new things that are connected; the real hockey stick of adoption and opportunity is using new capabilities such as Low Energy Bluetooth in ways to differentiate each of our respective businesses."

> "The real hockey stick of adoption and opportunity is using new capabilities such as Low Energy Bluetooth in ways to differentiate each of our respective businesses." Kevin Flowers, Coca-Cola Enterprises

The IoT learning curve will resemble that of the PC and mobile communication tools. Many firms initially failed to perceive the value in equipping employees with Internet access or in furnishing them with mobile phones. In contrast, the insight Coca-Cola Enterprises gained from deploying mobile phones to employees has proved invaluable.

Kevin notes: "The myth in the smart phone generation was it was about the data you can push. Rather it is the data you can pull into the company that creates strong value. We gained so much insight during the mobile generation that we will apply those same key learnings to the IoT generation at a much stronger cadence."

Kevin is pondering how to use Red Tag in the world of consumer engagement: "We don't know what world will look like after Red Tag is enabled for marketing and consumer shopping engagement—we are still figuring out the business use cases."

As one example, he is experimenting with augmented reality mobile apps, such as one that helps storeowners visualize how a Coca-Cola cooler will look when it is installed in their store. "We are putting apps in the hands of customers, leveraging them for better engagement. The future is how can we better our world—our partnerships and suppliers and customers?"

Kevin defines a connected world as one in which everyone and everything is linked. "We are not focusing on just doing our own digital strategy, but also linking things together. Our API strategy has significantly opened more information for our business ecosystem."

Kevin maintains that Red Tag can "IoT-enable" any environment and do so cost-effectively. Further, a Thingalytics platform approach creates an environment that is conducive to experimenting with the data generated by Red Tag.

This is one of the key factors underlying the IoT: The killer apps will emerge from experimenting.

Social Media for Machines

Social media has dramatically transformed people's lives. Only a decade or so ago if your son or daughter went away to college, you would have to rely on their (hopefully) weekly calls home to find out how they were faring. Today, you can see your kids on Facebook, follow them on Twitter, and look at photos of them with their new friends on Instagram. Their data flows to you, so you can see what is going on at any time.

Machines are becoming increasingly like people. They are equipped with tools that allow them to communicate with the outside world. The problem is that these machines are not connected, asserts Audi Lucas, Director of Connected Products at multinational consulting company Wipro. They are like college students without social media. Audi is working to change that.

Audi contends that machines are doing the same thing as college students are; specifically, they are streaming data out. "Every minute or thirty seconds they transmit what's going on into this fire hose with massive amounts of data. The problem is that most companies are not equipped with the tools to listen to, or understand, data at that volume."

Moreover, even the companies that monitor this data don't do so more than once a day. They may have developed algorithms to spot exceptions, or they run analytics to determine where failures are occurring and then notify a human to address the problems.

"Machines have been generating alarms for a long time," Audi notes. "But the algos [algorithms] are stale; they were often created before the product was released by someone who couldn't even imagine every scenario."

Audi contends that this paradigm should be modernized so that the data streaming from the machines is collected, preferably in the cloud, and then algorithms tweaked and allowed to evolve over time. Thus, if the company detects a new problem, then it can develop a new algo.

Audi wants to take machines out of their "remote service" Dark Ages past and bring them into the bright light of smart manufacturing. His quest started when he was working for a large multinational device manufacturer. In 2007, the firm moved him into a role developing the service strategy for new product development, which was much more technically demanding for the service technicians than the older mechanical systems. He quickly recognized that his overriding challenge was to get things connected, to be able to utilize knowledge-based diagnostics.

The company's standard practice was to assign a single technician to service all of the company's different products. Unfortunately, as these products became more complex, the technicians became less capable. "Some had problems using a laptop, never mind an IT-driven product line."

To counter this deficiency, Audi needed to centralize the company knowledge base, thereby enabling the techs who knew certain products to reach out and touch customers without the need for travel. In the traditional model, a service tech could spend a week fixing a problem, but he or she did not share this knowledge with other techs. Audi's solution was to station a skilled tech at the help desk, where he or she could diagnose the problem by using data sent by the machines to the central cloud-based system. This innovation reduced what had been a five-day diagnostic stint to a few hours. In addition, diagnostic history details would be stored in the centralized database that other techs could access.

In 2010 Audi joined GE as Service Systems Program Manager, where he worked for the Gas Engines division, which manufactures large power-generating engines. At the time GE was looking for someone to revolutionize its current remote service capabilities. "I was not in research and development, software or IT—I was in the part of the service business that was feeling the pain," explains Audi. He maintains, however, that this was an advantage due to the flexibility he and his team enjoyed. "When it comes to IoT systems, they are a different animal [from standard IT systems]. Your users are machines; imagine having 3,000 users on your system 24/7 forever." It was here that Audi started to explore a new frontier: connecting to products *after* they leave the warehouse in high resolution, providing better serviceability and enhancing GE's knowledge of their products.

As stated above, GE Gas Engines division manufactures large gas-powered engines used for small-scale power generation, from 0.5 to 10 megawatts—enough to power a small town. The largest of these generators is about the size of a school bus. These generators run factories and heat buildings and greenhouses, so they must be both efficient and reliable. As Audi explains: "There are two big things in power generation that are extremely important—reliability and efficiency. Reliability is crucial because the generators are not only for power but also for heat."

"If one generator fails, it can take down an entire manufacturing plant."

The operating standards for these generators are extremely high. Put simply, if one generator fails, it can take down an entire manufacturing plant. For example, Coca-Cola runs GE engines for all of its plants in Europe. If one fails and there is no heat, then Coke might be able to pull power off of the grid. This approach, however, is much more costly than using the GE "genset," or a generator which is located close to the end user.

Moreover, some plants do not even have the grid as backup. To quote Audi: "Imagine in middle of winter if one of the systems breaks. Reliability is a key here."

Because the GE engines are super-efficient in design, they are also complex. Audi compares them to Ferraris—highly efficient with plenty of alarms or sensors that could easily trip if they detect that something is malfunctioning. In reality the "problem" might not be immediately critical, or may be resolvable with a simple setting adjustment. In these cases the driver—or factory—wants the engine reset as quickly as possible.

In the case of a factory, particularly those in remote locations, dispatching a technician is not an option, speed-wise. "If you are lucky you could have one there in a few hours," states Audi. GE's solution? By constantly monitoring the GE engines, pulling the data from more than

> **By constantly monitoring the engines... GE could become proactive and remotely manage any issues as soon as — or sometimes even before — they come up.**

200 sensors into a central database and then creating algorithms around certain processes, GE could become proactive and remotely manage any issues as soon as—or sometimes even before—they come up.

The problem? "When I came in they had 25 different applications developed over time, there was a lot of home-grown stuff around service," Audi explains. His strategy was to pull together as much data as possible to create a single, integrated view of the assets. Then, rather than build a large-scale monolithic system, he and his team used a "mashup" approach to develop a system that anybody authorized could use by accessing the consolidated data from various systems of record.

First, however, he had to move GE away from its dial-up past, where customers had to dial into GE's virtual private network (VPN) to communicate with a service rep about their issues. "After ten years of VPNs and dial-up remote service, our connectivity penetration was only 10 percent of the install base. We really were not providing the full potential value in what users could do with that connection."

To resolve these inefficiencies, he developed a plan to connect all of GE's customers and distributors to the system, to collect their machines' data and push out solutions to them. However, accumulating all of this data and asking customers to allow GE to connect often led to the "What does this do for me?" syndrome. They had to identify their customers' and distributors' key pain points and give them some value back from allowing the connection to receive the data in return. Audi defines his success by the penetration of connectivity: "We got 90–95 percent of contracted engines online in under three years."

Smart Algos Find Their Bearings

The first algo GE's team wrote was formulated to deal with faulty generator bearings. One of GE's suppliers had switched bearings, and the service team was starting to notice premature failures, something many manufacturers have experienced. Audi recalls: "If the bearing failed completely, the stator [stationary part of a rotary system] inside the generator could start clanking around and could eat up the entire generator."

This was an expensive failure and, depending upon location, customers would have the additional cost and delay of getting a qualified technician onsite.

He adds: "This only occurred in a small portion of the fleet, but when it did it was very bad for the reputation of the company."

Audi's team wanted to be able to detect the bearing failure, then proactively call the customer and advise them of a possible issue. Meanwhile GE had time to send the improved replacement part and dispatch a technician. That way the bearing could be swapped out in a day or two, without causing damage to the entire generator and saving the customer substantial downtime.

The team wrote and implemented the algo, and Audi claims that the savings, simply from detecting that single failure, paid for his entire system development and implementation in less than a year.

No company likes to advertise when they have a product issue, of course, but the fact is that most production companies face these sorts of things all the time. "Take, for instance, the automotive industry; hardly a week goes by where there is not a recall of some type," Audi says, "But GE, under the leadership of CEO Jeff Immelt, had the vision to invest in advanced software and analytics technology, to help improve the impact to their customers, and has even gone further by adding value to the traditionally mechanical products. Imagine if the automotive industry would do that." (Tesla has, in fact, done just that with the connectivity and analytics of its cars. See Chapter 7.)

Audi's team then went on to create algos that detect cylinder valve wear issues, as well as predicting the lifetime of a sparkplug. "Sparkplugs are expensive; they sometimes cost more than $100 apiece. You want to know, if you run the engine for two months on 24 cylinders, will they last?"

So GE gave customers a view to how many hours were left on each plug. That way they could make sure they had enough hours left before doing a long run. This information saves customers money because they do not need to prematurely replace sparkplugs that still have life left in them.

Audi left GE in January 2014 for Wipro so that he could take these concepts to other companies. "GE was great, I was able to do a lot and get my hands dirty, but I could not take the solutions to other customers. Now I can go to lots of different customers."

His goal? "Connecting to products after they leave home. After they leave the warehouse, what is their life like? I don't try to second-guess the use-cases, though; I let the product and the users decide."

According to Audi, standard use-cases involve assessing the product's lifespan, how the customer uses the product and the product's reliability rate. However, he prefers to let the companies' users and stakeholders determine what they need to know *after* the product leaves home. "I tell our customers 'Don't try to come up with all the use cases and return on investment in the beginning. Often times the companies' users cannot even imagine the innovative things they can do with data like this until after they have seen the data."

To support this strategy, Audi cites the GE bearings algo—the one that paid for his system—which was "not even in the requirements. No one thought of it up front."

In sum, we can truly understand the connected world only by developing a Thingalytics platform and then helping the customer to understand what he or she is looking for.

Conclusions

Taking the Internet of Things beyond the hype and realizing its true value requires not just machines with sensors but also smart apps. It is these apps that consume and analyze the data, make smart decisions and initiate actions. Unfortunately we don't always know which apps are going to work. Consequently we need to take a platform approach—to allow for experimentation and refinement. That's the Thingalytics way! It is the approach that Coca-Cola, GE and Wipro have adopted.

Of course the hardware is really important. One key factor is cost. With Red Tag, for example, Coca-Cola took the visionary approach of developing a sensor-tagging technology to cost-effectively retrofit any non-IoT environment and make it IoT-enabled. Genius! Suddenly a legacy environment can become a state-of-the art, fast Big Data generator. GE Jenbacher adopted the strategy of augmenting expensive equipment with onboard sensors—which quickly paid for themselves when, combined with smart apps, they detected and prevented failures before they caused extensive damage. This capability also made servicing predictive, which in turn enabled the company to avoid expensive downtime.

The killer apps are still emerging. It seems clear, however, that inventory tracking and predictive maintenance are two revolutionary approaches that can save money and improve the customer experience. Other apps are emerging: Some will be winners, some won't. The key is to implement a Thingalytics platform approach, so we can explore rapidly executing, Big Data apps and identify and evolve the winners—to improve the customer experience, increase revenues and reduce costs.

3

Home Is Where the Smart Is

Meet George Jetson

In 1962, *The Jetsons* burst onto TV screens across America, showing us how the home of the future might look. *The Jetsons* is a cartoon set in 2062 (100 years after it was originally screened) featuring the Jetson family: George and Jane and their children Judy and Elroy, who live in Orbit City.

The way the show's writers envisioned the future—particularly the "smart home"—was somewhat prophetic. A robot maid, Rosie, sees to the family's housekeeping: Her chores are made easy thanks to the numerous smart conveniences located throughout the house. Meals are selected from an interactive menu screen and are prepared automatically by the family's smart kitchen. A conveyer belt ferries George Jetson into his smart bathroom, where robotic arms extend to brush his teeth. Flat-screen TVs and videophones are integrated throughout the home.

Believe it or not, the smart home has arrived in just under half the time the Jetsons writers had predicted! Although it is not exactly as they envisioned—there are no conveyer belts or robot arms in the bathroom yet—we do have robots that can clean floors; for example, iRobot's Roomba. Skype and other video conferencing tools are ubiquitous, making it possible to communicate about dinner with other family members who are not at home. And, as we shall see in this chapter, we are progressing towards smart kitchens that prepare meals for you, along with smart cable TVs that can alert you before a problem develops.

One innovation that the Jetsons creators did not anticipate was the integration of the Internet of Things and Thingalytics into the home. With Thingalytics, appliances are not just smart by themselves. Instead, they can produce data from sensors to communicate with other appliances. Further, centralized Thingalytics apps can make smart decisions based on this data. Equipping appliances with "senses" gives them "feelings" and the ability to call out for action or help. We can stay in the pub playing darts until the stove tells us our dinner is cooked. Similarly, we can turn down the heat automatically—when no one is home—to save power.

The opportunity to integrate the Internet of Things into our homes is so compelling that the goliaths of the computer industry have started to buy in. For example, Google acquired Nest[16] to obtain a competitive advantage in providing the hub of the smart home. Nest manufactures smart thermostats that, combined with apps, can automatically adjust based on rules pertaining to energy usage. The system can even learn patterns, such as what time people usually come home, to ensure the heating is on ahead of time. Meanwhile, Apple is promoting HomeKit—a development kit that enables families to control heating, lighting, security and other home appliances via a wearable Apple device.

> **The opportunity to integrate the Internet of Things into our homes is so compelling that the goliaths of the computer industry have started to buy in.**

If Apple and Google are piling in, then the smart home clearly is a huge opportunity. Many other companies whose products are traditionally found in the home, such as appliance manufacturers and cable TV providers, are incorporating this vision into their strategy. Here we tell the stories of two of them.

The Art of Smart Appliances

Fast food, pre-cooked meals, pizza delivery and eating out have overtaken home cooking over the past few decades. Doctors, health organizations and media have suggested that today's global obesity epidemic may be partly due to the dearth of home cooking.

---

[16] Marcus Wohlsen, Wired, January 14, 2014: "What Google Really Gets Out of Buying Nest for $3.2 Billion."

Food and agriculture author Michael Pollan[17] goes so far as to say that the best diet is: "Eat anything you want as long as you cook it yourself."

That said, finding the time to cook even the simplest of recipes can be difficult, given the demands of work and family. So, despite the rising popularity of celebrity chefs and cookery shows, few of us are brave enough to attempt the more difficult dishes. These shows can actually discourage people from trying to cook because they see professional chefs using professional equipment, which most of us do not possess.

The Internet of Things is changing all that. As kitchen appliances become increasingly connected, sensors can do everything from tell you when to turn the temperature down on the oven to when to order new water filters for your refrigerator. They can even help to restore the art of cooking.

Imagine you are getting ready to cook a big family dinner for a special occasion. You already watched your favorite TV chef prepare a roast turkey, while baking a lemon meringue pie and roasting potatoes at the same time. It looked complicated, but doable. You have two ovens, you have the ingredients and you have the motivation (Mum's 80th birthday).

What you don't have is the experience. The recipe calls for the turkey to be cooked for 20 minutes at 450 degrees Fahrenheit, then at 350 degrees Fahrenheit for 20 minutes per pound or until the internal temperature is 165 degrees. Meanwhile, the pie crust has to go in a separate oven to bake at 375 degrees and then under the broiler after the meringue is added. The roast potatoes are to be cooked at 350 degrees when the pie is finished.

You want the potatoes to come out at the same time you are ready to carve the turkey. The pie needs to cool for a little while before it is served. In the meantime, you are chopping vegetables and setting the

---

[17] Michael Pollan, Daily Ticker, April 25, 2013, Aaron Task: "Home Cooking Will Solve America's Obesity Epidemic." http://finance.yahoo.com/blogs/daily-ticker/michael-pollan-home-cooking-solve-america-obesity-epidemic-174714334.html

table, and you forget to turn the temperature down on the oven with the turkey in it. Dinner is ruined, the house smells of charred meat and tempers are running as high as the oven temperatures.

Believe it or not, tech people are developing ideas for new kitchen appliances that will be able to help you to cook that complicated meal, and more. Applying Thingalytics to connected appliances means that your cooker is not just helpful; it can also send information back to its manufacturer so that the appliance evolves based on your needs.

"The Internet of Things opens up ideas for the future," asserts Jakob From, Vice President of IT for Electrolux North America.

Electrolux already offers ovens that self-adjust the temperature, remove cooking smells and provide "probes" to measure the temperature of the dish. What Jakob is especially excited about are the possibilities for connected appliances going forward; in particular, ovens and microwaves.

"There is a trend toward living and eating healthier," explains Jakob, "which is feeding smart home innovation. And cooking is a big part of that. If a TV chef appears on screen and tells you 'Now I'm adjusting the temp to crisp up the skin,' it makes you feel more a part of the cooking process."

Electrolux manufactures the sophisticated cooking appliances, but how can they connect to the Internet and various other media for a fully interactive experience? Jakob believes that openness and collaboration are the keys to offering consumers the maximum benefit and ease of use from the Internet of Things.

To further this goal, Electrolux is participating in the Alljoyn[18] Project, an open source project initially developed by Qualcomm Innovation Center and hosted by the Linux Foundation's All Seen Alliance[19], which works to make connected products and software applications interoperable. This initiative has more than 70 member

---

[18] www.alljoyn.org
[19] www.allseenalliance.org

companies—including consumer electronics manufacturers, home appliance makers, retailers and software companies—all striving to enable the Things in IoT to work together.

Predictive maintenance could also apply to the home. Using predictive analysis on the large amounts of data generated by the IoT will one day make it possible to notify the consumer that a component might break within a specified time. Manufacturers could then provide the option of a proactive repair to keep the appliance functioning without interruption.

The data also gives the manufacturers a richer ability to analyze the behavior patterns of troublesome types of components. Manufacturers can identify the serial numbers, determine which batch they were produced in, and detect patterns to determine where the weakness occurred.

Going further, having appliances feeding data to the manufacturer means that, if something does break, the service engineers will be better equipped to know which part is broken. This—in turn—will increase the likelihood that the appliance will be repaired in a single visit, thus improving the consumer experience.

Jakob believes the IoT and connected appliances are giving Electrolux an even higher profile: "It is propelling us into the forefront of cool products; we are much more in people's minds."

> **"Maybe one day the food industry and smart appliance industry and health insurance industry will get together to solve the world's obesity problems." Jakob From, Electrolux**

Finally, by embracing open source ecosystems, connected appliances may even solve some of the world's problems. "Maybe one day the food industry and smart appliance industry and health insurance industry will get together to solve the world's obesity problems," Jakob muses.

Sentient Television

The television is often the entertainment center of the home; its hypnotic power ensnares viewers of all ages. In many parts of the world, particularly in the United States, cable and satellite TV providers have traditionally dominated the market. The Internet is threatening this model, however, and the Internet of Things and Thingalytics will take this challenge to the next level.

The cable television industry has to reinvent itself continually in order to stay relevant. It faces massive challenges by disruptive technologies, from streaming movies and programs on tablets and laptops to cheap, wireless-enabled devices for watching shows on your TV set.

In 2008, Cox Communications, the third-largest cable company in the United States, was confronted with a major shift in its business climate. Technology was changing, new players such as AT&T and Verizon had entered the cable delivery business and the global recession had hit. Cable TV subscriptions were one of the first things cash-strapped people cancelled.

Cox had to claw back subscribers and stop people from going over to Internet Protocol (IP)-based services, or "cutting the cord." To accomplish this goal the company had to greatly discount its services and create and manage new solutions, all the while taking care to stay compliant with draconian industry regulations.

Bruce Beeco, Principal Architect for Cox Communications, emphasizes that the recession hit hard: "It took us four years to get our baseline back, and we had to get more creative to grow further."

Cox provides smart-home technology to 7 million homes, and it prides itself on its award-winning service. Customer service is a familiar concept to Bruce, who has been in telecommunications since 2000, when he left the banking world. He claims that telecommunications and banking have a lot in common: "Both are service industries with similar challenges."

To address the new cable environment, Cox is becoming entirely digital and is moving customers off traditional analog. Bruce explains: "Cox will start converting its customers to all digital during the summer of 2015."

> Cox maintains that the advantage of moving from analog to digital is huge.

Cox maintains that the advantage of moving from analog to digital is huge. "For each analog channel converted, we can now provide multiple HD channels with extended features, such as interactive television," says Bruce. This means that Cox can move forward with its plans to offer a gigabit service to its customers.

Cox realized that, with its existing in-home presence, it could not only supply video, high-speed data and voice services, but also home security. "It is a natural fit; we have the pipe into your home already, so we just added video monitoring."

"We can offer complete remote management of your home," Bruce states. Cox is going beyond home monitoring, however, to take advantage of the wealth of data it can collect from its digital offerings.

"There is a proliferation of intelligent devices, and each one has data going through it," Bruce explains. He is already using real-time analytics to better understand the data the firm collects, and Cox has big plans for its future use. "This is the real-time piece, these devices are not dumb—they are communicating data back."

Bruce further contends that real-time analytics is critical to filtering through the "chatter noise" to ascertain what is valuable. "We can use it to determine the health of the offering; i.e., delivery. Or, we can use it to see what products customers are using, what programs they are viewing and the quality of the service delivery."

Also, because customers increasingly are "always on," bandwidth is more important than ever. "If they are downloading a movie, they only need the bandwidth for a few seconds," Bruce observes. Cox is utilizing real-time analytics to detect patterns in customer usage as well as problems and outages in real time. If 10 customers call in within five minutes, for example, Cox can detect the pattern, identify the problem and flash the message "There is a problem in your area" onto local sets. Cox correlates the customer problems with issues that might be happening in the network, and it can intelligently relate them. This capability saves on truck rolls—sending repair trucks out unnecessarily—and it deflects calls to call centers. "Cox has to reserve its workforce to manage real problems. Trucks do not have to go to a problem that doesn't exist; we could be using them for new sales or other more pressing issues."

Using real-time analytics, Cox can now find the small problems that used to fall through the cracks. If there are creeping problems with set top boxes or modems, the company can detect patterns and ID the issue. This approach not only saves money, it enhances Cox's reputation. "We are big on real-time and historic data, analyzing it to make it smarter—from minimizing truck rolls to optimizing delivery," Bruce asserts.

> Using real-time analytics, Cox can now find the small problems that used to fall through the cracks.

The next step is for Cox to determine which data is vital to improving its service. "People are afraid to throw away data, they don't know what is valuable," Bruce observes. "There is a lot of waste; they would rather keep the data than make a mistake."

Bruce wants to store the data and analyze it for patterns. "We dissect the data, see what they [customers] are calling about, the number of people calling about the same thing, the age of equipment and location."

Often times, problems with set top boxes and cable reception are caused by the customers themselves. If a customer moves a set top box and plugs the cables back in incorrectly, or if he or she leaves a magazine on top of the box that overheats it, Cox can detect the problem and avoid a truck roll. "We can slice, dice and track 100,000 metrics—their streets, their apps, the equipment model or vendor."

In the future, Cox wants to be able to learn more from its customers. What are they watching? When do they switch off the TV? Currently, set top boxes only indicate which channel the viewer is watching when the set is turned on. Bruce wants to learn more about viewers' patterns and behaviors to better customize their service. "If we could ID how you are watching TV, we could make recommendations for programs or movies you would like."

This information would also benefit Cox by enabling the company to measure advertising efficacy: "We want to see many eyeballs are watching. When did they change channels?" One compelling application here is the capability to offer advertisers much more targeted opportunities. For example, a regional university might want to run an ad for its MBA program, but only when a guaranteed 10,000 adults with an existing college degree are watching. This scenario is more appealing to an advertiser because they can run the ad only when the condition is true. A smart algorithm is watching and keeping track. Bruce cautions that all of these innovations will require increased bandwidth.

Other initiatives include "presence-based" applications that make it possible to locate and identify a computing device wherever it might be, as soon as the user connects to the network. "The presence component is the fastest-growing segment of the business," claims Bruce. "It is the next big area. We are forming alliances with other cable companies and giving customers free Wi-Fi when they travel." Once customers accept the terms of using the free Wi-Fi, then Cox can deliver dynamic advertising, targeted promotions and presence advertising to them.

Another initiative involves the so-called "second screen" in TV viewing. Non-TV devices such as iPads and smart phones can offer customized content that enhances the viewing experience and offers hands-on interactivity. These devices enable TV viewers to actively participate in their favorite sport or TV game show. Sports programming is a particularly ripe area for second screen viewing, because advertisers can sponsor dynamic ads, customized statistics and player facts, as well as social media interactivity. "An integrated second screen will offer advertisers an opportunity to add dynamic ads during events such as the Super Bowl, for example," states Bruce.

Cox Communications is a good example of a visionary company—one that takes perceived and real threats to its business and transforms them into opportunities using Thingalytics.

Bruce concludes that it is essential to stay relevant, because cable TV is so important to so many people: "As a network provider, there is no part of the industry that does not touch us every day."

Conclusions

Appliances and devices used in homes are becoming smarter and more connected. They can give us visibility into how the chores are being done, they can manage more complex instructions (such as stoves following complex recipes) and they can alert their manufacturers and owners when they are about to break down. Smart thermostats can adjust the heat by remote control and reduce energy usage by learning the home dwellers' behavioral patterns. Standards-based approaches, such as Alljoyn for connecting appliances and Apple HomeKit for controlling the home,

> ...Visibility of information from smart homes can educate service suppliers to plan better, improve their products, use less energy and fewer resources.

will enable sensored apps and devices to see inside and control the smart home. And this is just the start. Thingalytics in the home is going to exceed even the Jetsons' expectations!

An interesting side effect to the smart home is how the visibility of the information from multiple homes can educate service suppliers to plan better, improve their products, use less energy and fewer resources—and just generally make the world a better place. We have read (Cox Communications) how TV commercials can be much more targeted. In the future, for example, a retired lady might not have to watch commercials for diapers, but she might get more relevant commercials, such as a new pet food for her beloved cat. Moreover, that commercial will run only when a specific number of cat owners are watching. It is a Thingalytics-driven win-win-win for advertisers, consumers and cable networks.

Another innovation, the smart thermostat, is just one component of the "Internet of Energy." Gaining visibility into how homes are using energy enables power companies to waste less of the Earth's resources. The smart home will also have smart meters that can be connected to the energy markets—purchasing energy from the most cost-effective supplier and routing that energy the same way packets are routed on the Internet. This is end-to-end Thingalytics—from the power grid to suppliers to home.

We could move to a world where there are incentives, financial or otherwise, for customers to anonymously share information about activities in the home to third parties that can benefit from the knowledge derived. Going further, those third parties can provide insight to service providers outside the home. For example, data indicating that bad weather is keeping more people at home might translate into reduced demand for subway trains in the city—thus saving the city money and reducing our carbon footprint.

The smart home is causing many companies to evolve. For example, Apple started out as a computer company and then morphed into a media-player company through iTunes. Today it is involved in fashion (Apple Watch) and home automation (HomeKit). Google originally provided an Internet search engine and smart advertising. It now has fingers in many pies, including home automation (Nest) and self-driving cars—to get you to and from your smart home!

We could experience some interesting partnerships as the market dynamics evolve. Perhaps GE and Google will cooperate to provide end-to-end smart power from the utility to the home. Or, a long-anticipated collaboration between Apple and U.S. cable companies might create smarter, more personalized, mobile-enabled TV. Meanwhile, new killer apps will evolve that will make smart home services difficult to live without. One day, if you take a child from the next generation to an old fashioned, non-connected cabin in the Maine wilderness, she might well ask: "How do I switch this place on?"

> **New killer apps will evolve that will make smart home services difficult to live without.**

Take Two Smart Pills and Call Me in the Morning

The Smart Hospital

When I was an academic at Cambridge University in the 1990s, I super-vised a research project called "The Intelligent Hospital." The project explored how tracking the locations of doctors, nurses and patients—along with hospital procedures including vital signs, room sensors and drugs dispensed—would enable medical professionals to make better and more intelligent decisions. I am now starting to witness similar exciting smart applications being developed by technology companies that supply hospitals[20]. And, of course, the "smart" part in a smart hospital is driven by Thingalytics!

A smart hospital offers more advanced levels of customer experi-ence than a conventional hospital, and it can operate more efficiently. By tracking clinician locations, a smart hospital can map a new high-priority case to the nearest specialist or reroute the clinician from another case

A smart hospital offers more advanced levels of customer experience than a conventional hospital, and it can operate more efficiently.

based on its relative severity. Similarly, by tracking patient locations, a hospital can automatically detect a confused patient who has wandered out of his or her room and alert the nearest nurse.

Going further, the smart hospital complex can monitor and correlate multiple vital signs. For example, when a patient's blood pressure rises by a certain percentage, his temperature drops, and his heart rate falls to below a specified level—all within any five-minute window—an alarm is raised. Suppose these changes were caused by a new drug that was administered to the patient within the last hour and had an unexpected interaction with other medications the patient was taking.

---

[20] http://www.healthcaredesignmagazine.com/blogs/shandi-matambanadzo/keeping-pace-smart-hospitals

This information would trigger an automated recommendation to a nurse to stop the medication and consult a doctor. This multifactor system contrasts with individual alarms for each of the underlying conditions—which may not individually be significant and can end up having an effect on nurses called "alarm fatigue," in other words, the "cry wolf" effect. Humans can handle only so much input and so many crises per hour!

Another major feature of the smart hospital is the ability to constrain the spread of infectious diseases. For example, if a nurse leaves one patient's room and enters another without using the latex glove dispenser or the hand sanitizer within 15 seconds, then it is likely the nurse isn't going to complete the proper sanitizing procedures—and a potentially infectious disease could be spread. In this scenario the hospital can automatically raise a disease control alarm—which is not something a nurse wants to happen—thus encouraging the nurse to properly sanitize his or her hands immediately upon entering the room.

In all of the above scenarios and in the case studies below, data is created. Medical experts can utilize this data to analyze procedures and treatments to continually improve them, thus helping smart hospitals and doctors and nurses become even smarter. Thingalytics in action!

Hospital of the Future

In an operating room (OR) deep inside a major hospital, a procedure to implant a pacemaker is about to take place. The nurses are preparing the room and the patient, the doctor is scrubbing up and the technicians are adjusting dials and consulting with another professional.

That professional is not a doctor or a nurse; rather, he is the sales representative from the medical technology solutions company Medtronic. Why is a sales rep involved in an OR procedure? The reason is that the pacemaker was manufactured by Medtronic, and the sales rep is a trained clinical specialist who possesses in-depth product knowledge.

The physician arrives and confers with the sales rep. The rep enters some data into his laptop and sighs. He knows this is an important part of his job, but he would rather be doing what he loves best—selling.

This was also the conclusion that Paul Thompson, head of healthcare innovation for IT at Medtronic, arrived at after following sales reps in the field for three months. In his words: "We saw the inefficiencies as well as the changing hospital dynamics, and this triggered the idea for the Hospital of the Future."

Paul, who was a research scientist before deciding "IT was more interesting," was given a clean slate to collaborate with technology partner companies to create solutions that could add value. As he explains: "We did not try to tackle the whole hospital; rather, we focused on what would change the dynamics to benefit both the hospital and the patients."

> **"We did not try to tackle the whole hospital; rather, we focused on what would change the dynamics to benefit both the hospital and the patients." Paul Thompson, Medtronic**

One exciting project Medtronic has been involved in is the "artificial pancreas." This is an example of Thingalytics going on inside the body! Implanted sensors that analyze blood communicate with an implanted pump device that can administer the correct dose of insulin. This kind of closed-loop application can potentially revolutionize the lives of patients who suffer from some loss of organ function—in this case, people with type 1 diabetes.

Medtronic sales reps are highly specialized, testing and programming the devices as well as entering critical data and inventory information. According to Paul, "There are a lot of manual processes, so we decided to make them fully automated, so that everything is ready when the patient arrives in the OR."

Going further, Medtronic is personalizing the device experience for each patient, proactively. The company does not do this on its own, however. Paul explains: "We work in tandem with our partners in IT. We are the master integrator."

Medtronic develops a wealth of intelligent medical products ranging from internal heart monitors and defibrillators to spinal implants and brain implants that can ease tremors in Parkinson's patients. Paul's world focuses on leveraging the data around devices, systems and hospitals to help reduce the costs of healthcare. "Every country wants to cut the costs of healthcare," he contends. "We are doing it using smart devices and analytics."

Smart devices and analytics help make better use of doctors and nurses' time by reducing travel costs and getting the right people to the right place in time. Patients' costs are reduced by having their medical problems fixed early, before they require critical care. Hospital costs are reduced when the spread of diseases is minimized.

Reduced costs are not the only benefit generated by smart devices and analytics. Paul claims that by streamlining OR procedures, smart devices and analytics make a patient's experience easier. From the time patients arrive, they get more quality time with doctors, nurses and technicians. Also, doctors and nurses are better prepared for their tasks. "By the time the doctor walks in, he or she is ready to roll," Paul maintains.

Medtronic is also considering strategies to help hospitals manage patients with chronic diseases when they are outside the hospital. Specifically, technologies such as *telemedicine*—medical information exchanged from one site to another via two-way video, email, smart phones and other wireless tools and forms of telecommunications technology—enable patients to avoid costly and time-consuming hospital visits. Among other things, monitoring technology and alerts can inform caregivers or physicians whether a patient has taken his or her medications.

The interplay between Thingalytics and the Internet of Things comes into play here, as medical experts deploy more and more devices that can send reams of data to hospitals and Medtronic. Thingalytics can then help to make sense of all this data by analyzing it for patterns, good and bad, and identifying new efficiencies or business opportunities while avoiding potential threats.

"This is where the Internet of Things and healthcare come together," Paul asserts. Hospitals can utilize analytics to combine intelligence with patient alarms to determine whether a call is an actual emergency, thereby saving doctors and nurses from alarm fatigue. The use of smart devices combined with analytics can make everyone's life easier—in or out of the hospital.

Smart Disease Control

You do not want to catch Ebola. The Ebola virus kills approximately 70 percent of people who contract it, but not before it causes severe vomiting, diarrhea and bleeding. Unfortunately, there is no vaccination against Ebola. Hopefully, however, modern medical technology will help us win the battle against this deadly virus.

Medical experts assert that Ebola can be transmitted only by direct contact with bodily fluids from an infected person who is displaying symptoms or by handling a victim's corpse. Nevertheless, despite stringent controls, caregivers handling Ebola cases are being exposed to the virus.

Infectious disease control comes down to science combined with human diligence. Unfortunately, however, even the strictest of guidelines cannot ensure that Ebola will not spread. Because the United States has not enacted federal quarantine laws, a victim can slip through the international travel safety net. In addition, a single slip in the mandated routine of healthcare workers donning and removing personal protective equipment (PPE) after treating an Ebola patient can lead to contamination and infection.

The complicated and meticulous protocol for putting on and taking off PPE—including double rubber gloves, hazmat suits and respirators—was designed by the U.S. Centers for Disease Control and Prevention (CDC) and the World Health Organization (WHO). This protocol mandates a rigorous and repeated training system and a dedicated human "Ebola monitor." The rules are long and detailed, but they are essentially intended to ensure that caretakers do not expose any flesh when they are treating patients or removing PPE.

Infectious disease control comes down to science combined with human diligence.

Disease control is an area where Thingalytics technology and the Internet of Things can work together. Thingalytics makes intelligent monitoring and responses to the inputs from multiple networked sensors possible. In a "smart disease control" scenario, these sensors can even be worn on the skin, integrated into clothing or a building, or attached to medical probes. Intelligent software can monitor and correlate the data generated by these sensors to identify dangerous patterns. For example, if the sensors detect exposed flesh on a doctor before she goes into the patient's room, then they could trigger a series of events such as locking the patient's door to prevent the doctor from entering. At the same time another doctor would be summoned by text message so as not to endanger the patient.

In another scenario, hospitals could monitor patients, doctors and nurses for breaches in protocol. For example, if a nurse dealing with an Ebola patient removes her second pair of gloves incorrectly—allowing the patient's bodily fluids to touch her skin—an alarm could sound before she can touch her face and thus infect herself.

Thingalytics for smart disease control could ensure that all surfaces of an Ebola patient's room are thoroughly cleaned and send alerts if anything was missed. This function is critical because the Ebola virus can live on a dry surface such as a doorknob for several hours, according to the CDC.

Hospitals can also use Thingalytics to help deter the spread of Ebola by replaying events from the start of an infectious disease case. They can highlight all of the caregivers who were in contact with the patient, as well as all of the other individuals these caregivers came into contact with. Or, if an "at-risk" Ebola patient is detected outside an authorized area, then the nearest nurse or appropriate caregiver could be alerted.

The possibilities are endless for Thingalytics, from constraining the spread of Ebola and other infectious diseases to preventing bioterrorism. For example, a city government agency could be alerted if multiple health clinics in the area have prescribed drugs within the past few days that can be used to treat symptoms of bioterrorism. This could signal an imminent bioterrorism attack. Once alerted, the city would be better prepared to track the terrorists and prevent the attack.

Technology might not save the world, but it can help save a patient or a caregiver's life.

By using technology for smart disease control monitoring, clinics can begin to automate rules to determine breaches in protocol and to identify suspicious patterns. Immediate danger alerts can enable health officials to take the appropriate actions instantly to head off problems. This is one way to enhance the monumental human effort that goes into infectious disease control. Technology might not save the world, but it can help save a patient or a caregiver's life.

My Doctor Is a Robot

Throughout the world, there are many places that are hard or dangerous to reach and/or have poor medical coverage, particularly by medical specialists. The 2014 Ebola crisis in West Africa is one example. Thousands of cases of the deadly virus were reported in countries with critically low numbers of doctors per patient, including Liberia (just over 1 per 100,000), Sierra Leone (just over 2) and Guinea (10). To put these numbers into perspective, the United States has 245 doctors per 100,000 people, and Spain has 370, according to *The Economist*.[21]

In addition to the technologies we just discussed, another tool to help control the spread of infectious diseases like Ebola is robotics. Worcester Polytechnic Institute (WPI) in Massachusetts is looking to repurpose a manufacturing robot, Baxter, to help keep Ebola healthcare workers safe by removing their PPE for them.

Along the same lines, WPI, Texas A&M and the University of California, Berkeley, are working to repurpose existing disaster zone robots to focus on Ebola. Another robot WPI has begun adapting is the Autonomous Exploration Rover (Aero). Aero was originally designed for space exploration, but WPI believes it can be utilized for decontamination work. By adding sprayer tanks to the body of the robot, Ebola zone cleaners could operate the robot remotely, thereby avoiding the risk of infection.

Going further, medical robots could be utilized for purposes other than containing infectious diseases. Consider, for example, the battlefield. Troops on the front line frequently sustain injuries that require specialist care that is not available on site. And, perhaps a little further into the future, as humans spend more time in space, injuries and medical conditions could arise millions of miles from the nearest clinic! How can people in these circumstances receive quality medical care?

---

[21] www.economist.com/blogs/graphicdetail/2015/02/ebola-graphics

Using high-resolution video, a surgeon in a remote location can see the patient and manipulate surgical equipment locally. Also, by digitizing the surgeon's movements and transmitting them as data over a network, the surgeon can remotely control a robot surgeon. Through video, the surgeon receives immediate visual feedback. This capability can potentially scale the power of a surgical specialist many times—saving lives in far-flung locations without the need to travel there. As technology advances so that robot surgeons can become more autonomous, these robots can be programmed to handle simple injuries or to open and close a patient, thus freeing up the human specialist for more serious consultations. This arrangement derives more value from the human expert, enhances efficiency and creates the potential to help more patients.

Remote patients can be constantly monitored through a range of sensors, and the sensor outputs can be analyzed. As the utilization of these Thingalytics increases, remote surgeons can be intelligently contacted when complex scenarios occur. In a way, Thingalytics becomes the nurse by the bedside, raising the alarm and patching a video channel through to the relevant on-call expert, wherever he or she is located.

Plug-and-Play Medicine

Developing the Thingalytics-as-nurse theme, as healthcare costs spiral, hospitals increasingly need to treat patients from a distance whenever possible. Remote consultations, patient monitoring and advanced digital diagnosis are just some of the ways a smart hospital can use technology to improve patients' experiences—and keep them from making unnecessary trips to the hospital. As the costs of sensors and connectivity continue to drop and advances are made in wireless, mobility, cloud computing, streaming analytics and big memory caching, these technologies are becoming more viable.

Moreover, as monitoring devices become an integral component of the healthcare industry, it makes sense that these devices should also become a part of a patient's daily life. Enter wearable technology—the next Big Thing in monitoring. The medical industry is an enthusiastic early adopter of these technologies. From sports bracelets that can monitor a patient's pulse to Google-designed contact lenses[22] that can measure diabetics' blood sugar levels, technology is increasingly penetrating the medical field.

For example, Apple has designed a platform for app developers called HealthKit that can be used with Apple's hardware to collect health information and transmit it to doctors. HealthKit pulls information from other medical apps and devices to make it more useful. The information is then stored in a centralized location that no one can access without the user's permission.

According to Tech Times[23], doctors at Stanford University Hospital are already working with Apple to track blood sugar levels in children with type 1 diabetes. These children will be given an iPod touch to monitor their glucose levels in between their scheduled doctor's visits. In addition, Google and the drug company Novartis are partnering to develop contact lenses that monitor blood sugar. Novartis's Alcon eye care unit plans to create products to track glucose levels using Google's prototype smart contact lens, which utilizes miniature sensors and a radio antenna thinner than a human hair.

Remote monitoring can go even further. For example, sensors can be swallowed or installed inside the body to check vital signs and send alerts to the doctor if they detect an abnormality. Smart pill dispensers can remind people to take their medications at the right times. And, webcams can be used to monitor and stream what is happening on the ground to doctors in remote locations, thus saving time and money. An example is

---

[22] Mark Scott, NYT, July 15, 2014: "Novartis Joins With Google to Develop Contact Lens That Monitors Blood Sugar." http://www.nytimes.com/2014/07/16/business/international/novartis-joins-with-google-to-develop-contact-lens-to-monitor-blood-sugar.html?_r=0
[23] Lauren Keating, Tech Times, September 15, 2014: "Apple's HealthKit will start medical trials." http://www.techtimes.com/articles/15614/20140915/apple-s-healthkit-will-start-medical-trials.htm

New Jersey cardiologist Jordan Safirstein, who uses Google Glass to video-stream surgical operations to his students, who can view them live on their smartphones or tablets. This technology enables his cardiac fellows to learn about problematic situations as he encounters them in surgery.

> **Thingalytics analysis could detect that you are likely to suffer a massive heart attack the next day.**

Sensors worn on the skin can potentially reduce healthcare costs—for example, by saving visits to the doctor's office—and even prolong lives. Imagine, for example, that your personal wearable sensors are continuously analyzed when you are sleeping. Thingalytics analysis could detect that you are likely to suffer a massive heart attack the next day—based on your heart behavior, pulse, blood pressure and temperature. It is probably worth skipping the business meeting you were going to attend and checking yourself into a specialist clinic. A horrible thought, but better than being dead!

I fully anticipate that a combination of wearable and implantable sensors and drug dispensers will radically prolong lives. Perhaps even immortality is within our grasp—although after 200 years you will probably be more cyborg than person!

The Hospital's Digital Fabric

It is not just the inside of the hospital building that can benefit from Thingalytics, but the very fabric of the building can also take advantage. The number of healthcare facilities that have incorporated smart technology has increased, and this trend inevitably will continue. From RFID and real-time location services to smart rooms and systems that monitor, control, and adapt for energy efficiency, an abundance of developments is being rolled out to the market.

The world of possibility and innovation has grown by leaps and bounds in the design and construction sector as well as in the medical industry. Because the current build timeline spans several years, certain processes and products are becoming passé before the hospital is even completed. If owners want to keep up with the very latest in technologies that will benefit patients and save money, they could create a nightmare for architects and construction managers as change orders start to pile up to accommodate up-to-the-minute trends. If these developments can save lives, however, then the extra effort is worth it.

Healthcare facilities are under pressure to transform themselves into more ecologically friendly buildings. In the same vein, patients and employees are more tech-savvy, and they are demanding the most current products on the market that will add to quality of care and/or reduce time spent in the hospital.

> Innovative ideas can help a cash-strapped hospital achieve better-quality care, both through the design of the physical space and technological advances in medical equipment.

Granted, incorporating all of the very latest tech ideas can be an expensive undertaking that not all facilities can afford, or even need to implement right away (things like automated guided vehicles, for example). However, there are innovative ideas out there that can help a cash-strapped hospital achieve better-quality care, both through the design of the physical space and technological advances in medical equipment.

The infrastructure of the smart hospital, from both a physical and technological standpoint, must be as flexible as possible to accommodate the rapidly changing future.

The Patient Experience

Imagine a seriously ill young boy who has to go for tests at a children's hospital. He has been to this hospital before, too many times, and the fear on his face is clearly visible. He is terrified of strangers and needles and noisy CT scans. His parents are stressed about his state of mind as well as his health. They worry for his safety if they have to leave him there alone for any length of time.

Now imagine a different kind of hospital, where the young boy is greeted by well-known faces. When he gets to his room he recognizes it as the same cozy room in which he stayed during his previous visits. The TV is on, tuned to the Cartoon Network. The boy rushes in to make sure his favorite video game is still loaded onto the console. It is! And the websites he bookmarked for a class project on frogs are still on the computer. And his friends' Skype numbers are there!

The room temperature is preset to 80 degrees, because the boy is easily chilled, and the blinds are wide open so he can see other children playing outside. He feels instantly at home, and his parents relax a little. They know he is going to be safe and comfortable and well attended by medical staff.

This is not fantasy. It is a hospital of the future. Nemours Children's Hospital (NCH) is an internationally recognized full pediatric healthcare facility located in Orlando, Florida. Nemours uses Thingalytics technology to weave together hospital systems that traditionally do not communicate with one another. At Nemours, hospital surveillance, RFID, facilities, clinical scheduling and other systems are all working together, behind the scenes, to ensure their patients' safety and security. Using patients' personal and medical data, the hospital created a "smart building" that ensures a comforting, customized experience for young patients and their families. The result is a healthcare environment that is safer and more engaging for its young patients, yet efficient and informed for the doctors, nurses and other support staff.

Consider, for example, the benefits generated by RFID badging. When a caregiver walks into the boy's room, a sensor reads the badge. The caregiver's picture—pulled from the hospital's HR system—will then display on the TV inside the room. This system lets Mom know that the person matches the badge, and it lets the hospital know which caregiver is with which patients.

Thingalytics technology also helps enable intersystem communication and automation for security events. The security systems, facilities systems and clinical systems collaborate through automated event-driven processes. So, for example, if a newborn baby is removed from its cot by anyone other than authorized personnel or its parents, an alert is sent immediately to security staff, possibly preventing a kidnapping. If a child has an urgent medical event, then the staff is notified as soon as the attack begins.

This smart hospital is just one example of the power of Thingalytics. By integrating patient records with clinical, administrative and security systems, Thingalytics enables Nemours to be the most responsive facility it can be and to provide a secure, healing environment.

Conclusions

Thingalytics is a key driver in the quest for smart hospitals. By continuously analyzing locations, vital signs, drugs administered, room sensors and many other inputs and personalizing them to the medical situations in the hospital, Thingalytics can enable hospitals to provide a level of care previously unimagined, while reducing healthcare costs.

Making buildings smart can enhance energy efficiency as well as improve customer service through location-aware personalization. Going further, wearable and implantable technology is going to revolutionize healthcare—moving closer to a model in which Thingalytics monitors your health continuously, reducing the number of expensive and unnecessary clinic visits. Through Thingalytics we may achieve the promise of eternal life—as we continuously predict and fix health problems—although clearly this will lead to the necessity to colonize other planets. Otherwise, how will we all fit on Earth?

5

I'm the Chairman of the Board

Algorithms: The Brains of Thingalytics

Algorithms are everywhere. They help you find friends on Facebook and decide which films you might enjoy on Netflix. They assist you in everyday Google searches. A Wall Street trading algo can watch how the market behaves to spot opportunities and then execute trading decisions in less than a millisecond, to ensure that you buy or sell at the best price. An algo can sniff out and email relevant jobs to you that are advertised online. There is even an algo that can predict the likelihood of an oncoming vehicle running a red traffic light!

Algorithms are the brains of Thingalytics. Algorithms feed on sensory inputs and give birth to analysis, recommendations, decisions and actions. Yet, without quality input they are in the dark. However, when they are fed with the rich inputs from streaming data and the Internet of Things, they drive a smarter world.

He Works Hard for the Money

Chairman VITAL takes his job very seriously. He was recently elected to the board of the Hong-Kong-based venture capital firm Deep Knowledge Ventures.

DKV focuses on drugs for age-related diseases and regenerative medicine projects, and it wants VITAL to help the board make important investment decisions. The decisions taken by the board—ranging from companies that use computers[24] to research drugs to firms with systems that can select personalized cancer therapies—can make or break DKV.

VITAL works day and night helping the company make the right investment choices. But, there is no fear that he will burn out or that his home life will suffer. Because VITAL—short for Validating Investment Tool for Advancing Life Sciences—is an algorithm. For the first time

---

[24] Rob Wiley, Business Insider, May 14, 2014: "A Venture Capital Firm Just Named An Algorithm To Its Board Of Directors—Here's What It Actually Does." http://www.businessinsider.com/Vital-named-to-board-2014-5#ixzz38O2IT98M

in known history, a mathematical formula has been given a seat on a corporate board of directors.

This is no small thing. Even if the VITAL experiment fails, the fact that an investment company took an algorithm seriously enough to give it board status indicates just how far these formulae have come. From Amazon deciding which books you might like to Match.com choosing your ideal life partner, algorithms have become ubiquitous.

Algorithms work something like the human brain in that they take a set of rules and procedures and then use them to make and execute decisions. Algos tell a computer what to do and when and how to do it. They enable companies to add intelligence to their processes, mining data for meaningful patterns that can turn into golden nuggets. They can even replace human beings, taking away the drudge work of trawling the markets for breaking news or sorting through reams of data to find patterns. As algorithms become more intelligent they can be used for far-reaching decision making that can further impact the fate of human beings.

> As algorithms become more intelligent they can be used for far-reaching decision making that can further impact the fate of human beings.

In VITAL's case, he is being asked to make decisions by scanning data on prospective companies—analyzing their financing, clinical trials, intellectual property and previous funding—and then deciding whether they represent a sound investment. He then gets to vote on the final investment decisions. His decisions can affect every board member, partner and shareholder in DKV, as well as the companies that DKV invests in.

So, what if VITAL messes up and tips the scale on a vote for a company that eventually fails? Does that make him a bad chairman? Or does it make him an evil computer trying to take over the world?

The answer is no. Most algos turn bad only because of lapses by the human beings who design them. Careful planning and assessment of possible unintended consequences can prevent an algo from making expensive mistakes.

In fact, VITAL could be a better board member than his colleagues. It is not as if human board members did a great job at managing their companies pre-2008 (or even post-2008). One tongue-in-cheek survey on the Internet claimed that a potted plant would make a better board member than a human. Significantly, algos came in second. (To protect the innocent, we will not name the plant.) Whatever its ultimate success, VITAL could be the precursor for many more algos on corporate boards throughout the world.

The Case of the Mysteriously Expensive Book

In April 2011 Michael Eisen, an evolutionary biologist at UC Berkeley, and one of his postdoctoral researchers noticed that a book on Amazon—Peter Lawrence's *The Making of a Fly*, a classic work in developmental biology—was priced at more than $1.7 million (plus $3.99 shipping). The next day they checked again and discovered the price had jumped to $2.8 million. Over the course of the next few days, before anyone at Amazon noticed, the price rose to nearly $24 million (plus $3.99 shipping).

Eisen and his colleague realized that an interaction of pricing algorithms was causing this debacle, so they reverse-engineered the logic. Eisen hypothesized that the algorithm for one vendor, Profnath, that did not actually own the book, recognized that a competitive vendor, Bordeebook, had the book in stock. Consequently, the algorithm offered the book from Profnath at roughly 1.3 times the Bordeebook price—to build in some profit for Profnath. However, in parallel, Bordeebook's algorithm, unaware that this was going on, decided Bordeebook was offering the book far too cheaply relative to Profnath. Consequently, it re-priced the book to 0.9983 times Profnath's price. Consequently—and unknown to the companies or to Amazon—the two algorithms engaged in an escalating price war, continuously driving up the price until it reached into the millions.

Amazon, the world's largest online retailer, is a store run by algorithms. Algorithms decide the prices of many wares, they determine what you might like to buy next, they calculate the best way to stock the shelves in their many warehouses and they process your orders. In addition, many Amazon retailers use algorithms to help make the pricing of their products smarter and more adaptive. These retailers can automatically adjust their prices relative to other vendors when they detect price changes.

For example, an algorithm operating on behalf of Bates Booksellers might detect that ABC Books has lowered their price on my book *Thingalytics* to undercut them. Bates Booksellers can program its algorithm to re-price the book at 99 percent of the ABC Books' price—thus ensuring it will never be beaten on price. *Thingalytics* will be flying off the shelves!

Money Machines

One major area in which algorithms are used is automating the trading process within financial markets. You probably know that this has become a controversial issue in the press, in the public eye and in government. The term "high-frequency trading" (HFT) has become demonized in the popular conscience. It is associated with high profits and greed, and it is often cited as a cause for the May 2010 Flash Crash. (However, none of these accusations have been proved, and there is much evidence to the contrary.)

HFT algos have even made it into books. One nonfiction work by business storyteller-extraordinaire Michael Lewis—his 2014 book *Flash Boys: A Wall Street Revolt*[25]—threw the media into a tizzy. Lewis's book

---

[25] Published by W. W. Norton & Company; 1 edition (March 31, 2014)

took some potshots at HFT, claiming the stock market is "rigged" by Wall Street insiders and exchanges. Lewis's book appeared a couple of years after Robert Harris's 2011 novel *The Fear Index,* in which advanced trading algorithms go out of control and try to take over the world.

This idea is a capital markets equivalent of Skynet in the *Terminator* films—in which a military defense algorithm becomes sentient and subsequently triggers a nuclear war. Of course Skynet then follows up by creating machines designed to eradicate the remaining humans. We will tackle the risks of trading algorithms and how to police them in Chapter 6, "RoboCops: Smarter than the Average Criminal." For now, let's focus on the opportunities and benefits offered by algorithms.

HFT actually involves applying smart mathematics very quickly to streaming market data to spot patterns, such as very short-term pricing anomalies between two or more products or liquidity sources—so-called "statistical arbitrage." HFT algorithms are programmed for profit. They fit with the popular media image of a trading algorithm: an autonomous brain that makes trading decisions and executes them. Of course, HFT algorithms know when to trade, and even sometimes what to trade, but they still require human input to give them these capabilities.

> **High-frequency trading algorithms know when to trade, and sometimes what to trade, but they still require human input to give them these capabilities.**

The "high-frequency" part refers to the speed of trading electronically. The algos must keep up with myriad high-frequency streams of data, make decisions based on patterns in that data that indicate possible trading opportunities and automatically place and manage the orders in the market. HFT algos are typically used in banks' proprietary trading groups, hedge funds and independent proprietary trading firms.

In the past couple of years HFT firms have increasingly incorporated news feeds into their algos. The reasoning is that firms can trade automatically on news sentiment before a human trader can react.

Examples are:

- Responding first to economic releases, such as selling the dollar if the nonfarm payrolls results are worse than expected.

- Responding first to world news, such as buying the Swiss franc and gold on news of a war.

- Responding first to unexpected weather events, such as buying orange juice futures on news that a hurricane is predicted to hit the Florida orange crop.

The algos can also correlate and respond to patterns; for example, the way that news historically impacts price movements.

HFT is just one application of algorithms in the trading world. There are also execution algorithms—less glamorous workhorses, typically run by brokers, that help buy-side clients such as fund managers move in and out of large positions. Execution algorithms break down large orders and feed them into the market over a specified period of time. The idea is to minimize the impact of large orders on the market. Pumping a large order directly into the market exposes the trader's intention to the market and can affect either the supply or the demand—moving the price too far up or down.

To avoid this disruption, the algorithm splits up the order over time using a mathematical model. Another goal of execution algorithms is to achieve a benchmarked price; that is, an appropriate average price for the market conditions. Examples of execution algorithms are the volume-weighted average price (VWAP) and "market-participation algos."

Algorithmic techniques have also been used in the real-time pricing of instruments such as bonds, options and foreign exchange. Traditional pricing techniques use slower-moving pricing analytics and fundamentals to price instruments. In contrast, today's higher-frequency algorithmic techniques can enhance these pricing algorithms based on an up-to-the-millisecond view from the market, including the available liquidity and price trends.

In all forms of algo trading, and particularly in HFT, speed is vital for success. Specifically, trading groups are concerned with *end-to-end latency*; that is, the time interval for the entire trading process, which encompasses the following steps:

- The market data is generated at the trading venue(s)
- This data is delivered to an algo
- An algo makes a decision based on the data
- The orders are placed and filled at the venue(s)

When several firms are competing for the same opportunity, the one with the lowest latency wins. There is a lot more to algos and high-frequency trading than just latency, but latency is clearly critical.

Lowering the latency in market data feeds, order execution and the algorithmic trading engines themselves has become a key focus. Sometimes algorithms are actually installed next to or in the facilities of a trading venue. Some firms have become passionate about the physics of reducing latency, making the actual wire connection over which market data and orders are transmitted as short as possible! As algorithms become more complex and handle more markets, the focus will shift to the "smarts" of algorithms and away from wire lengths.

Marrying Humans and Algorithms

Despite what we encounter in popular fiction, we are actually a long way from sentient algorithms that try to wipe out humanity. It is useful, however, to consider how the integration of algorithms into financial markets has transformed the roles of human traders over the past 20 years. In fact, examining the role of algorithms in trading is an excellent microcosm through which to study the ways algorithms are used, the issues surrounding their use and the directions in which they are headed.

The degree to which algorithms have modified the fabric of the financial markets industry is extraordinary. Until the 1980s trading was conducted on the floor of traditional exchanges—where a lot of shouting and hand waving went into the trading process. Much of the trading was based on the traders' intuition and experience. When markets became electronic, traders had to adjust to sitting behind computer terminals, watching real-time market data on multiple screens and using the same intuition and experience to manually spot patterns and enter orders using a keyboard. This development made markets much faster-moving.

Connecting trading algorithms to the markets took speed to a new level and totally redefined the dynamics. Some of the intuition and experience that traders had used in certain circumstances was being packaged as an algorithm. Consequently, traders were forced to become high-level coordinators of a set of algorithms—knowing when to start a particular algorithm, which key thresholds to monitor and when to become manually involved. Some traders didn't make this transition well. Less-advanced traders were completely replaced by algorithms. More-advanced traders, however, became vastly more productive than they could be when using only their brain and body.

From eyeball to brain, it can take a human trader 30 milliseconds to spot a trading pattern. Once the brain has processed the pattern the next step is to act on it, which involves sending signals to the trader's hands to enter the order. This step can take a second or two. By the time all of this activity has transpired, an algorithm could have detected thousands of patterns and placed thousands of orders. Going further, thousands of algorithms multiply this capability by thousands of times.

> **An algorithm doesn't need coffee, lunch or bathroom breaks.**

An algorithm doesn't need coffee, lunch or bathroom breaks. However, algorithms don't have the same level of intuition and experience as human traders—so often the human trader becomes the master of thousands of algorithms. The algorithms are more like slaves than sentient rulers of the world. Will algorithms ever replace human traders completely? We'll address that question later.

It's All Relative

Trading is highly competitive. Opportunities come into existence and are spotted, and the market becomes more efficient as traders pile on. One of the key competitive advantages in the world of trading is *first mover advantage*: Identifying a new opportunity and moving on it. This process also involves recognizing when this opportunity is no longer working and moving on. The Aite Group[26] reports that the average shelf life of a trading algorithm is three months. This is certain to become even briefer!

The next generation of algorithms will not wait to be told what, when and how to trade. They will be programmed to calculate what to trade and the strategy to trade it, and they will continuously self-evolve to remain profitable and outwit competitors. We are closer than ever to the era of such self-learning algorithms. Some advanced firms are experimenting with these tools using massively scaled statistical correlations to try to predict emerging trading relationships between instruments, which could then serve as the basis of a profitable trading strategy. The firm then tracks those correlations to ensure they are still valid.

Consider the technique of *genetic tuning*, in which many thousands of permutations of algorithms are run in parallel and fed with real

---

[26] www.aitegroup.com

market data, but are not necessarily trading live in the market. Imagine a trading algorithm with six parameters. Through genetic evolution, we might "learn" the optimal values of those parameters and make that algorithm live. Over time, the algo may become less profitable, at which point we can deactivate it and replace it with a new one. This model of algo trading allows self-evolving systems to discover profitable opportunities through evolutionary processes, with some seeding and guidance by human experts.

When you hear of complex and sophisticated algorithms being used for trading, you probably think of a JPMorgan Chase or a Goldman Sachs. In fact, there is a whole ecosystem of smaller trading firms that are also utilizing cutting-edge algorithms to make money. One of these firms is Relative Technologies (RT), a small Australian commodity trading advisor that trades global futures and foreign exchange on electronic marketplaces, using automated trading methods. RT's strategies involve utilizing various statistical methods over short periods of time to generate consistent returns with manageable volatility.

> There is a whole ecosystem of smaller trading firms that are utilizing cutting-edge algorithms to make money.

Relative Technologies Chief Investment Officer Hugh McGuire maintains that using algorithms to trade keeps the company light and nimble. In his words: "You don't need a lot of manpower to trade futures."

Relative Technologies utilizes automated statistical strategies to exploit price anomalies of futures listed on the CME Group exchanges. This primarily means spread trading. Hugh explains: "We look for correlation between two futures markets—for example wheat and soybeans on CME—over two to three years."

Hugh is exploring a number of trading techniques, including genetic algorithms. His objective is to identify new profitable correlations and to recognize when existing correlations change. "The longer the correlation lasts, the more others jump on it," Hugh asserts. "If there is a big move, it can be a danger sign. Sometimes it is best to stop trading if the pattern breaks down." He adds: "One change can be a sign of more changes to come."

No matter how valuable algorithms are, at some point they stop laying the golden eggs. "Then it is time to find different hidden nuggets of gold to trade upon," Hugh explains, "and hope you hit a vein." Some algos have been "very dependable," running for six months with "not too many losing days." Lately, however, the trading opportunities are harder to mine.

Despite the enormous impact of algos, Hugh contends that they have not been a destabilizing force in the marketplace. Rather, "It is heaps better now, the average investor is way better off than in the days of specialists."

Specialists, or designated market makers, on many U.S. exchanges provided liquidity and helped to maintain a "fair and orderly" market, by stepping in themselves when buyers and sellers weren't available, according to Bloomberg.

Specialists began to disappear when exchanges started pricing stocks in penny increments in 2001, squeezing profit out of the bid-ask spread, and, increasingly, as the markets became electronic[27].

Finally, being able to trade in different markets is key, says Hugh: "You need diversity for stability."

ANZ and the Rapidly Changing FX Market

The global foreign exchange (FX) market is huge. It dwarfs all other markets in terms of trading volumes and the amount of money that changes hands. Dozens of currencies are crossed each day to the tune of more than $5 trillion, and that number is rising. Significantly, the

---

[27] Nina Mehta, Bloomberg, September 3, 2010: "SEC Questions Trading Crusade as Market Makers Disappear." http://www.bloomberg.com/news/2010-09-13/sec-second-guesses-its-stock-trading-crusade-as-u-s-market-makers-vanish.html

FX market is not a single exchange. Rather, it comprises a network of electronic trading platforms, brokers, banks, corporations, funds and retail clients. FX is massive, and it is complicated.

Traditionally, FX was traded by hundreds of bank dealers who priced to hundreds of clients. It was all about relationships, built up over the years between the banks and their clients. In the late 1990s, as FX trading evolved, the emergence of currency trading platforms such as ICAP's EBS and Reuters Dealing, as well as bank portals such as State Street's Currenex, changed the dynamics. Dealers did not understand how to access all of the pools of liquidity, and it was difficult for them to see all of the prices or depth of the liquidity.

ANZ, a visionary bank based in Sydney, Australia, took a deeper look at the FX markets and decided that a smart FX aggregation algorithm was the best solution to this problem. The underlying belief is that the best prices could be located on any of a multitude of FX trading venues: EBS, Reuters, Hotspot and Currenex, along with platforms from all of the major dealer banks.

The smart aggregation algorithm can monitor the data streaming from all of these platforms and create a single view of best bids and best offers for each currency pair. A currency pair describes the cross rate for two currencies; for example, Australia Dollar/U.S. Dollar (AUD/USD), Euro/U.S. Dollar (EUR/USD), and so on. Several of these currency pairs are internationally supported instruments. However, a smart aggregator can also create "synthetic" pairs in real time, such as British Pound / Mexican Peso, by continuously combining the cross rates for the different currencies.

"We decided that the traditional deal-by-deal method of trading was not very efficient, and we began to build an aggregator," recounts Luke Marriott, Global Head of Wholesale FX at ANZ. "We had experience from the derivatives market, where you have a portfolio of risk that looks at the underlying correlations. What we needed was the computational capacity to do this for FX."

ANZ had created different trading engines for Northern and Southern Hemisphere currencies, which the bank had to merge into a unified pricing and distribution engine. "This is how our e-business in FX evolved," Luke explains.

ANZ's aggregated e-commerce platform enabled the bank to get back into the FX game, which the global banks had encroached upon. The bank's technical investment enabled them to ascend from 43rd place in the Euromoney FX Survey[28] into the top 20 in just three years. Luke explains: "We invested in technology in order to facilitate trading in the deepest pools of liquidity."

"Technology is progressing faster than regulation, that's for sure."

Luke Marriott, ANZ.

He observes that regulators often lack knowledge about the markets and technology: "This is an education for them. Technology is progressing faster than regulation, that's for sure."

Luke further contends that regulators seem intent upon making FX more like an exchange-traded product. "But there are too many pools of liquidity for one central exchange," he concludes. "There are always costs involved with making a market fair. And we keep coming back to aggregation."

Social Algorithms

Algorithms are widely used inside social media such as dating websites, which pair up people based on similar interests, age, location and other details. One of my followers on Twitter, with whom I regularly exchange ideas, once tweeted: "Ten years ago I met my amazing wife on Match. com. She was rated a mere 50 percent match." In this particular case, I'd give the algorithm an A-. It made an excellent suggestion, but it assessed

---

[28] http://www.euromoney.com/Article/3338848/Euromoney-FX-survey-2014-results-revealed.html

compatibility based only on a few surface criteria. The remaining 50 percent of the work to determine compatibility had to be done the old-fashioned way.

When financial services algorithms meet social media, a whole new dynamic is added. Algorithms can monitor social media feeds to gauge market sentiment and act upon news, instantaneously trading instruments worth billions of dollars, thus causing the market to spike or drop. This scenario might sound like popular fiction, but it is not. Twitter mining is becoming the next big thing in algorithmic trading as firms employ sentiment analysis to qualify and quantify the emotional chatter around a particular market. Traders then gauge whether the feelings for a particular stock or commodity are negative or positive, and they can utilize that information to make trading decisions.

The problem with the widespread availability of social media is that it can be misused. Consider the following scenarios:

- On April 23, 2013, hackers hijacked the Associated Press's @APTwitterfeed and tweeted that bombs had exploded at the White House, injuring President Barack Obama. As a result, the Dow Jones Industrial Average fell more than 150 points, the price of crude oil plummeted and U.S. bond yields dropped, briefly wiping $121 billion off the value of companies in the S&P 500 index before recovering minutes later.

- In October 2010, U.S. prosecutors nabbed a gang who allegedly used Facebook and Twitter social networking sites to tout stocks in a classic 'pump-and-dump' fraud totaling roughly $7 million. The fraud was uncovered during a cocaine-trafficking probe, according to Reuters.

Trading using information from social networks is a hazardous game: Danger lurks when a piece of news or trading advice can be posted, tweeted and retweeted online without filters. A piece of spurious, market-moving information can be bounced around the world and traded upon by a human being or an algorithm before anyone can say "What the heck…?"

The safest and most effective form of Thingalytics social analysis involves using the entire Internet of Things as a tool for "global consciousness." Rather than focus on particular tweets or postings, which can be manipulated, traders should focus instead on aggregating the sentiment across all postings. One example of this technique involves utilizing data from the 100 billion+ Google searches[29] to understand economic sentiment.

Central banks, including the Bank of England[30], use available data from Google search and other social networks as a benchmark to understand how citizens feel about the economy. Are they searching for new cars or looking for jobs? They use this data as a key input into deciding whether to raise or lower interest rates. Google search data represents a more accurate and up-to-date pulse of popular sentiments than a survey does.

> The Bank of England uses available data from Google search and other social networks as a benchmark to understand how citizens feel about the economy.

In the coming years we are going to see more algorithms using sentiment as a feed. This process could involve assessing the sentiment of a shop full of people, based on video analysis to see whether they are smiling, and adjusting the store's temperature or prices accordingly. Alternatively, it could involve assessing the sentiment of the capital markets to determine which direction they will move in. Or, it could

---

[29] http://www.businessweek.com/news/2012-08-01/your-119-billion-google-searches-now-a-central-bank-tool
[30] Ed Conway, Sky News, December 27, 2014: "Bank Of England To Monitor Social Networks." http://news.sky.com/story/1397985/bank-of-england-to-monitor-social-networks

involve determining the sentiment of a country to predict whether the people will revolt. More and more, algorithms will be used by marketers and governments to take the pulse of the population. A key point here: All of these Thingalytics algorithms are fed with social behavior data.

Conclusions

The fear today is that algorithms could be overused, removing human creativity from the decision-making process. They could turn us humans into mush-minded creatures who can't be bothered to make our own choices. If algorithms are as powerful as some critics contend, couldn't they one day replace humans with artificial intelligence? The question is not a new one.

More than a dozen years ago, Stephen Hawking, a globally recognized physicist and cosmologist, warned that if humans were not genetically enhanced they would not be able to compete with artificial intelligence. He predicted that the increasing sophistication of computer technology is likely to outstrip human intelligence at some point in the future. In a September 2001 interview with the German magazine *Focus*, Hawking explained: "In contrast with our intellect, computers double their performance every 18 months. So the danger is real that they could develop

> "The development of full artificial intelligence could spell the end of the human race." Professor Stephen Hawking.

intelligence and take over the world." In December, 2014 he repeated his fears to the BBC[31]: "The development of full artificial intelligence could spell the end of the human race."

With all due respect to Professor Hawking, who is one of my heroes from my alma mater Cambridge University, I must disagree. Yes, human

---

[31] Rory Clellan-Jones, BBC: "Stephen Hawking warns artificial intelligence could end mankind." http://www.bbc.com/news/technology-30290540

decisions may be slower than algorithms. Significantly, however, human intuition is often the "secret sauce" in decision management—including validating that certain algorithmic decisions make sense. The appropriate combination of smart algorithms plus human oversight and intuition can be hugely beneficial to the responsive business.

Of course, as the number of algorithms that make recommendations increases exponentially, the danger exists that technology can make us lazy. Blindly following an algorithm can be like driving into a lake because your GPS told you to (true story[32]!). If you do not use intelligence—human or artificial—to establish the correct parameters of an algorithm, then the algorithm can take you down the wrong path.

Relying solely on human inputs to make decisions can make a business slow and unresponsive. Conversely, relying exclusively on algorithms, without any human oversight, can lead to your business algos making crazy decisions before anyone can stop them. Merging the two elements in the right way, however, can create an adaptive, learning business that moves before competitors do and continuously adjusts to changing market conditions.

Algorithms are the smarts behind Thingalytics. In the next ten years we will witness an exponential rise in algorithms, playing the role of the invisible angel, the digital concierge and the 21st century slave! Algorithms have transformed capital markets into a lightning-fast, intelligent, self-optimizing environment. Coupled with the emergence of the Internet of Things, their food source—streaming Big Data—is about to expand off the charts.

Science fiction of the 1960s focused on robots transforming the world. In reality, unseen algorithms that add intelligence will transform companies into smart businesses.

---

[32] Lauren Hansen, The Week, May 7, 2013: "8 drivers who blindly followed their GPS into disaster." http://theweek.com/article/index/243813/8-drivers-who-blindly-followed-their-gps-into-disaster

RoboCops: Smarter than the Average Criminal

Dumb Criminals, Smart Technology

The media frequently portray white-collar criminals as highly intelligent individuals who use sophisticated codes or secret algorithms to commit fraud and manipulate markets. The truth is, most of their activities are fairly amateurish—yet they manage to get away with them for months or even years.

What has been missing in financial services markets is a kind of RoboCop. Not the part-human, part-robot of the 1987 film, but a regulatory policing system that monitors a combination of human and market behaviors to detect patterns that signal fraud or error.

Consider this scenario: A cadre of interest rate traders conspires to manipulate the London Interbank Offered Rate (LIBOR), using instant messaging platforms and chat rooms where they barely try to hide their efforts. This activity goes on for about seven years before someone blows the whistle[33].

Or this one: In a private messaging chat room, foreign exchange (FX) traders who call themselves the "Three Musketeers[34]" conspire to move the FX benchmark price by "double-teaming" (a sports term meaning using two players to defend against an opposing player) and "whacking" (offering below) the market. They carry out this scheme for about four years before regulators catch on.

And, the story doesn't end here. We read multiple news stories about a "fat-fingered" algorithmic order—where a trader enters a wrong number or an extra zero into the trading system. The worst reported case took $1 trillion out of the stock market in just a few minutes. We hear about a drunken broker who enters his office in the middle of the night to make

---

[33] Christopher Alessi, and Mohammed Aly Sergie, Council for Foreign Relations, December 5, 2013: "Understanding the LIBOR Scandal." http://www.cfr.org/united-kingdom/understanding-LIBOR-scandal/p28729
[34] Gavin Finch and Liam Vaughan, Bloomberg, November 13, 2014: "'Cartell' Chat Room Traders Boasted of Whacking FX Market." http://www.bloomberg.com/news/2014-11-13/-cartell-chat-room-traders-boasted-of-whacking-fx-market.html

an illicit crude oil trade that costs his company millions of dollars. We wince in sympathy with regulators as we read about absurdly blatant insider trading schemes.

All of these crimes, errors and frauds were carried out more or less in plain sight. What does this tell us? It indicates that financial services firms have not taken adequate steps to monitor trades and traders to spot aberrant behavior and anomalous trades.

Trade monitoring has improved, thanks to a crackdown on high-frequency trading (HFT) by regulators. More can be done and needs to be done, however, as investors grow weary of dark pool shenanigans (where traders can deal in private) and flash crashes.

The process of monitoring the behaviors of traders and other participants is in its infancy. Advances in audio and video monitoring will help banks detect unusual human behaviors; for example, if a trader fails to take a vacation for a year or appears abnormally nervous when speaking on his cellphone outside his office building.

Combining trade and data monitoring with surveillance of the human side of financial markets can alert firms to potential fraud or problems with automated trading.

Combining trade and data monitoring with surveillance of the human side of financial markets can alert firms to potential fraud and to problems with automated trading. Patterns can be discovered and crimes can be traced when monitoring and surveillance meet Thingalytics to form our own market RoboCop.

Flash Crash: First Chink in the Armor

At approximately 2:45 pm Eastern time on May 6, 2010, Scott O'Malia noticed something unusual. He was walking by a television screen at Philadelphia's Constitution Hall when he saw a chart—one that displayed the steep decline that characterizes a market crash. Because Scott was in a museum, his immediate reaction was that he was looking at some historical stock market event. He then looked again and realized the scenario was not historical; rather, it was happening at that moment. The Dow Jones Industrial Average (DJIA) had plummeted by nearly 1,000 points. Stunned, he stopped and checked his BlackBerry to find an explanation. "I said to myself: 'What happened? What has caused this? Was it political, economic, security?'" It was important that Scott know because, as one of the commissioners[35] at the Commodities Futures Trading Commission (CFTC), a U.S. regulatory agency, it was his job to know.

Amazingly, Scott was unable to find any news about the incident on his smart phone. Because he was chaperoning his daughter's school trip to the museum, he was responsible for the children, so he had to move on.

Back at the CFTC's offices at 1155 21st Street, NW in Washington, D.C., Scott's teams were frantically working with CME Group, a major exchange that the CFTC regulates, while watching as several price points were hit and limits were triggered. The crash had spread to the equities markets and the DJIA and Standard and Poor's (S&P) 500 indexes were dropping like stones.

"The team was trying to understand what the [futures] relationships were with stocks while everything was plummeting, plus trying to gather information and explain what had happened," Scott recalls.

Just as open-mouthed traders were absorbing the catastrophic drop, the market recovered almost completely. The entire episode had run its course in less than 30 minutes.

Later that day, Scott was on the school bus when he received a call from the office of CFTC Chairman Gary Gensler, who was also trying to get to the bottom of this mini-crash. As Scott explains: "It took weeks before we were able to understand the confluence of events that put us into that situation."

---

[35] O'Malia left the CFTC in July, 2014 and is now the Chief Executive of the International Swaps and Derivatives Association (ISDA).

Dubbed the *flash crash* by the market, the event created a global domino effect, crashing stock markets throughout the world. The crash left scorch marks that scarred the reputation of the bulwark U.S. stock market and damaged already fragile investor confidence. Weeks, even months, of investigations unearthed one very important piece of information: Regulators were unprepared and ill-equipped to deal with this kind of event.

What Do You Do with a Drunken Trader?

High-speed markets that lack adequate supervision, including real-time monitoring and surveillance, are at risk of even more severe consequences than flash crashes. Without trying to overstate the issue, in the most extreme circumstances abusive practices could be considered algorithmic terrorism. The concern is that a well-funded terrorist organization will use these tactics to manipulate or cripple the market. So much of our economy is underpinned by electronic trading that protecting the market is more important than guarding Fort Knox.

Both before and after the flash crash there have been dozens of mini-crashes, fat-fingered trading errors, and even cases of downright fraud.

Both before and after the flash crash there have been dozens of mini-crashes, fat-fingered trading errors, and even cases of downright fraud. The list appears to grow almost daily.

Consider the following scenarios:

- In January 2008, high-profile rogue trader Jerôme Kerviel[36] woke up the world to the fact that trading without proper risk

---

[36] Lizzie Davies, The Guardian, October 5, 2010: "French rogue trader Jérôme Kerviel sentenced to jail and €4.9bn fine." http://www.theguardian.com/business/2010/oct/05/jerome-kerviel-jail-sentence

controls and supervisory oversight could lead to unintended consequences. In this case the consequences were losses of almost €5 billion for the bank Société Générale, because Kerviel had knowledge of—and abused—risk-management systems at the bank to hide losses.

- In June 2009 Steven Perkins[37], a broker in the London office of PVM Oil Futures, got drunk and, in the middle of the night, took on a 7.0 million-barrel long position in oil futures. Perkins eventually was fined and banned from the industry, but not before he cost PVM somewhere in the vicinity of $10 million (after they unwound the $500+ million position).

- On February 3, 2010, HFT firm Infinium[38] Capital Management's brand-new trading algorithm malfunctioned and racked up a million-dollar loss in about a second. The new algorithm went live for four minutes just before markets closed and fired off between 2,000 and 3,000 orders per second before being shut down. Although the entire episode lasted less than a minute, that was enough time for the algorithm to generate an eight-fold spike in trading volumes. In turn, this spike caused the oil price to surge $1 before sliding $5 over the course of the next two days.

---

[37] Rowena Mason, The Telegraph, June 30, 2010: "How a broker spent $520m in a drunken stupor and moved the global oil price." http://www.telegraph.co.uk/finance/newsbysector/energy/oilandgas/7862246/How-a-broker-spent-520m-in-a-drunken-stupor-and-moved-the-global-oil-price.html

[38] Jonathan Spicer, Reuters, November 25, 2011: "High-frequency firm fined for trading malfunctions." http://www.reuters.com/article/2011/11/25/us-cme-infinium-fine-idUSTRE7AO1Q820111125

- In June 2010, one of Deutsche Bank's trading algorithms in Japan[39] went into an infinite loop and took out a $183 billion stock sell position. Fortunately, the bank was able to manually unwind most of this position, but not before it gave the Nikkei stock market index a flash crash scare. Following this incident Deutsche Bank shut down its Japan-based proprietary trading group. Better pre-trade testing and a risk firewall to prevent aberrant trades from going to market could have averted this catastrophe.

- In July 2010, a currency-trading execution algorithm at Rabobank—an international enterprise headquartered in The Netherlands—malfunctioned and placed a $3 billion FX order[40]. This action caused the UK pound / US dollar currency trade rate to drop by 1 percent. Better testing, real-time risk rules and trade monitoring could have prevented this incident.

- On March 31, 2011, a mini-flash crash[41] nearly wiped out ten Focus Morningstar exchange-traded funds (ETFs) that had just been launched on NASDAQ OMX and NYSE Euronext. Fortunately, the exchanges were quicker off the mark than on the May 6 flash crash, and they cancelled some of the trades. However, other ETFs tumbled by 98 percent before circuit breakers kicked in. The culprit appears to have been a human

---

[39] Shingo Kawamoto and Finbarr Flynn, Bloomberg, July 16, 2010: "Deutsche Bank to Close Three-Person Desk in Japan Following Trading Error." http://www.bloomberg.com/news/2010-07-16/deutsche-bank-said-to-close-japanese-desk-responsible-for-trading-error.html

[40] Adil Siddiqui, Forex Magnates, August 7, 2012: "The Glitch Strikes Again." http://forexmagnates.com/the-glitch-strikes-again/

[41] Rodrigo Campos, Reuters, March 31, 2011: "Plunge in 10 ETFs triggers 'flash crash' memories." http://www.reuters.com/article/2011/03/31/usa-markets-etfs-idUSN3128578120110331

being with fat fingers. An ETF market maker (liquidity provider), Knight Capital, was the culprit.

- On May 5, 2011, the crude oil market experienced its second-largest daily drop ever[42] when trading algorithms repeatedly triggered sell-stops. This time there was no fat finger and no Greek tragedy-style news as in the 2010 flash crash. The $13 drop in the price of Brent crude was almost unprecedented, yet it made few headlines. Declines in oil prices are like increases in equities prices—good news for most people.

- On June 8, 2011, an alleged fat finger wiped 8 percent off natural gas prices on NYMEX[43] in an after-hours trade made in Asia. The natural gas market recovered almost immediately, but not before some savvy traders realized what had happened and jumped in to buy and profit from the mistake.

Knight Capital and the London Whale

Following these events, two other cases were reported that rocked the foundations of capital markets trading. On August 1, 2012, a rogue command triggered a buy order for 140 different stocks on the NYSE. As we mentioned in the Introduction, this action launched a sequence of events that took down the brokerage firm Knight Capital.

The firm had installed new software[44] that conflicted with old code, which was supposed to have been deleted. This conflict caused a flood

---

[42] Matthew Robinson, Reuters, May 5, 2011: "Oil crashes 10 percent in record rout." http://www.reuters.com/article/2011/05/05/us-markets-oil-idUSTRE7446 BH20110505

[43] Nanex, June 8, 2011: "Strange Days." http://www.nanex.net/StrangeDays/ 06082011.html

[44] John McCrank, Reuters, October 17, 2012: "Knight Capital posts $389.9 million loss on trading glitch." http://www.reuters.com/article/2012/10/17/us-knight capital-results-idUSBRE89G0HI20121017

of orders to surge onto the NYSE without the benefit of volume caps. The erroneous piece of code cost the company $440 million—roughly $10 million per minute.

Knight Capital teetered on the edge of insolvency as its executives desperately sought funding from white knights in other areas[45]. Four days after suffering its massive losses, the firm was saved by Getco LLC, Blackstone Group LP, Stephens, Inc. and Jefferies Group, Inc., as well as Stifel and TD Ameritrade, which put together a $400-million rescue package.

Then, in February 2012, the chief investment office of the London branch of JPMorgan Chase experienced a traumatic episode that made Knight Capital's losses look inconsequential. A Chase trader named Bruno Iksil (nicknamed the "London Whale") took a spectacularly large position on credit derivatives that ended up costing the bank $6.2 billion, plus a fine of $920 million. The London Whale allegedly had mismarked some of the losses to cover up their magnitude, something U.S. prosecutors called securities fraud.

According to *The New York Times*, "One serious defect in the risk evaluation of Iksil's position was that its limit was folded into the aggregate risk of the unit's entire portfolio. In other words, Iksil could continue to increase the position without triggering alarms[46]." In addition, the firm had implemented a new value-at-risk model in January 2012, which engendered a false sense of security among regulators and banks.

The rogue's gallery of fraudsters discussed above should have served as a warning to other banks that traders can falsify trades and massage

---

[45] Michael J. de la Merced and Nathaniel Popper, NY Times Dealbook, August 5, 2012: "Knight Capital Reaches Rescue Deal With Investor Group." http://dealbook.nytimes.com/2012/08/05/knight-said-in-talks-to-obtain-new-capital/
[46] Susan Dominus, New York Times, October 3, 2012: "The Woman Who Took the Fall for JPMorgan Chase." http://www.nytimes.com/2012/10/07/magazine/ina-drew-jamie-dimon-jpmorgan-chase.html?pagewanted=all&_r=0

internal systems to hide their actions. Apparently this did not happen. We can add to that gallery two more scoundrels.

The first, Kweku Adoboli[47], was an equities trader at UBS whose fraudulent hiding of bad trades cost the bank more than $2 billion. Perhaps the most upsetting aspect of the Adoboli scandal was that his crimes became known only after he reportedly blew the whistle on himself. He was able to hide his losses for months because he had extensive knowledge of and access to middle- and back-office systems.

The second figure is Jon Corzine[48], the former CEO of MF Global—as well as a former New Jersey senator and governor—under whose supervision $1.2 billion in customer money from presumably segregated accounts disappeared. MF Global's misconduct was even more egregious than Adoboli's because the firm allegedly filched money from customers' brokerage accounts to pay off loans and margin calls on a large-scale European debt bet.

As serious as these violations were, the LIBOR and FX benchmarking scandals mentioned in the Introduction were many times more costly. The fines[49] alone on the six banks involved in the FX fixing totaled $4.3 billion. Finally, reports that surfaced late in 2014 maintained that price fixing has been going on in the metals market as well[50]. One wonders what revelations are next.

---

[47] Peter Walker, The Guardian, November 20, 2012: "UBS rogue trader Kweku Adoboli jailed over 'UK's biggest fraud'." http://www.theguardian.com/uk/2012/nov/20/ubs-trader-kweku-adoboli-jailed-fraud

[48] Bruce Bialosky, National Review Online, February 5, 2013: "Corzine's Crime of the Century." http://www.nationalreview.com/articles/339811/corzine-s-crime-century-bruce-bialosky

[49] Reuters, November 12, 2014: "Regulators fine global banks $4.3 billion in currency investigation." http://www.reuters.com/article/2014/11/12/us-banks-forex-settlement-cftc-idUSKCN0IW0E520141112

[50] BBC, November 25, 2014: "HSBC and Goldman sued for allegedly fixing metal price." http://www.bbc.com/news/business-30209544

Managing the risk connected to algorithms that go wild or to dealers who add another zero to their orders is one part of the overall puzzle. Catching outright fraud, from insider trading to manipulation of markets and internal trading systems, is another. We now turn to that topic.

Revenge of the New Market Structure

Almost all of the rogue trader and fraud events discussed in this chapter came about because of computerized trading. Automated trading was accelerated in 2005 when the Securities and Exchange Commission (SEC) passed a set of rules known as the Regulation National Market System (Reg NMS) that created a new market structure in the United States. Reg NMS was designed to give investors the best possible price when dealing in stocks, even if that price was not on the exchange that received the order. As a result, new exchanges and other venues such as alternative trading systems (ATSs) and electronic communications networks (ECNs) popped up like weeds. At one point there were as many as 60 venues for trading equities, options and futures in the United States.

Traders soon realized that these rules created attractive new opportunities. For example, traders could take advantage of incremental gaps between prices on different exchanges by using computer models to conduct high-frequency trading. Increasingly, brokers and traders employed algorithms to execute their trading strategies and to enable HFT. Significantly, these practices were regulated only lightly, if at all.

> **Clever trading companies built complex algorithms to buy and sell futures, shares and FX contracts in the blink of an eye.**

Clever trading companies built complex algorithms to buy and sell futures, shares and FX contracts in the blink of an eye. All of this evolution was implemented with little thought to the possible repercussions in the event a trader made a mistake.

Thus it was that on May 6, 2010, when mutual fund Waddell & Reed[51] in Kansas entered a $4.1 billion sell order in E-mini S&P 500 futures contracts on the CME, the reverberations were felt throughout the marketplace. As a buy-side participant, Waddell & Reed was using an automated algorithm through its broker to slice up the large order into smaller batches, in order to minimize the impact on the market. Apparently, however, the parameters of the algorithm were badly defined. Specifically, they made the batches too large, thus putting almost the entire order into play at once.

The size of the computerized sell order sparked a totally human panic in the market on a day when fear already was in the air. The magnitude of the Greek debt crisis had become widely publicized, and sentiment was becoming bearish. This panic was exacerbated by algorithmic trading strategies and HFT. The result was an unprecedented 5 percent drop in the DJIA within minutes, wiping out $1 trillion in market value before the market recovered. That a simple mistake could take the market down so fast was unthinkable—but it happened.

> **The size of Waddell & Reed's computerized sell order sparked a totally human panic in the market on a day when fear already was in the air.**

CFTC's Scott O'Malia maintains that on the infamous day of the flash crash the market moved so quickly because the price drop triggered get-outs in trading algorithms. He noted: "Everybody said 'I can't explain it; my machines can't explain it,' so they pulled out. This further exacerbated the problem because there was no buy side liquidity."

---

[51] Dealbook, May 17, 2010: "Waddell Defends Its Trades During Flash Crash." http://dealbook.nytimes.com/2010/05/17/waddell-distances-itself-from-flash-crash/

When the CME's stop logic finally kicked in and generated a five-second pause in trading, investors realized that the world had not ended and that the dip was a potential buying opportunity. Scott says: "The buy side came back in, and the market snapped back."

But, what if it hadn't? Although the flash crash was a mere blip in the grand scheme of things, it signaled fundamental flaws in both the new market structure and the ability of U.S. regulators to manage this kind of issue.

The CFTC had to reconstruct the day using whatever the exchanges could offer: data, the trading profiles of different entities and how these entities were conducting their trades at the time. It was an all-encompassing, time-consuming affair that ate up vast amounts of resources. Not surprisingly, finger pointing was rampant.

Critics alternately blamed the futures market and the equities market. Eventually, a consensus emerged that the flaws were distributed equally, although the equities side became painfully aware that the lack of price limits and circuit breakers on its side caused further problems. Scott reflects: "There were some structural problems in the equity market in that some of these things did not respond and did not come back."

In the following days an overwhelming sense of frustration emerged in response to the CFTC's failure to propose a complete answer as to why the flash crash happened. "I wasn't going to say 'Let's come up with *an* answer,'" Scott says. "We had to get the right one, find out what was really the problem. If it takes us longer, then so be it."

Ultimately, the commissioners did find a satisfactory explanation. However, the quest was long and difficult, and the lack of monitoring and surveillance technology sorely hindered the regulator's efforts. Significantly, Scott was not surprised that the CFTC struggled so hard and so long with this issue. As he later acknowledged: "Long before the flash crash, it was clear to me this agency did not have the resources."

Hope for the Market

Mark Hope is a compliance officer based in London who has worked at several major global banks. He describes his job as being "there to help ensure that the bank conducts its business in an appropriate manner."

Mark has witnessed a radical change in attitudes since 2008 as various crises have unfolded. During these years banks have moved from being generally less engaged with compliance to being more proactive. One fundamental reason for this transformation is the heavy fines levied against offenders.

The foreign exchange benchmark manipulation, for example, cost banks dearly. Mark notes: "These days, an average foreign exchange spot desk will make $50–$80-million profit a year. In the recent incident several banks were fined by regulators $300–$375 million apiece. That's potentially a few years' worth of income; they may as well have stayed at home!"

The banks involved in LIBOR manipulation were off-the-scale big. "The total fines for one firm [alone] hit $1 billion. It completely wiped out their profits."

It should not come as a surprise, then, that smart compliance is now at the top of the agenda in capital markets institutions!

Mark argues that problems related to compliance were exacerbated by the failure of many firms to invest in this area during the boom years. These firms employ a number of legacy systems that don't talk to one another and surveillance systems that monitor only specific aspects of a business. A modern smart surveillance system ideally should track *everything*—which means it needs to tap into all of these systems.

Although LIBOR was a "black swan" incident (high-profile, difficult to prevent[52]), Mark maintains: "No one thought LIBOR was a particularly high-risk area, but no one was thinking about the potential

---

[52] http://en.wikipedia.org/wiki/Black_swan_theory

consequences of abusing it. Many people purported to know LIBOR was being manipulated; from the looks of it, in hindsight, everyone did it. Then someone blew the whistle."

Anticipating black swans requires both people and systems. One key strategy is to use smart analytics to detect outliers—to recognize that something out of the ordinary is happening. However, this approach doesn't work in all situations, particularly when the ordinary pattern includes the manipulation. Mark explains: "Theoretically, if traders have been manipulating something for years and then they stop, *that* would be the unusual behavior!"

Nevertheless, Mark is convinced that, despite all of the reputation-damaging incidents we have considered, financial markets are a power for good. For example: "In a simplistic way of looking at it, an average bloke, his wife and two kids want to go to Disney World in Florida. They buy their plane ticket in U.K. pounds from British Airways. However, British Airways pays for fuel in U.S. dollars, and they probably bought the plane in U.S. dollars, not to mention the various multicurrency obligations BA has around the world. Without financial markets offering compelling foreign exchange hedging opportunities, the ticket prices could be far higher. You don't really get the impression that anyone outside the market realizes this."

Mark adds that you can expand this example to the multitude of methods that companies all over the world use to balance their books, from FX and commodity products to interest rate derivatives: "If you suddenly removed their ability to hedge effectively, the price impact this would have on all manner of goods and services could be huge."

Ultimately, then, the industry must implement smart surveillance systems to try to avoid the bad things, like huge fines, and take advantage of the good things, like lower costs for financial services, which can reduce the price of these services for customers. In the following section I explain how they can do this.

The Seven Pillars of Thingalytics' Trade Surveillance

We have discussed major problems that plague the trading world: flash crashes, rogue traders, market manipulators, insider trades, fat fingers and wild algorithms. Now, let us consider how Thingalytics can address these problems.

> What the next generation of trade surveillance and risk systems needs is a crystal ball.

Trade surveillance is in need of a radical modernization. We need to identify early warning signs to anticipate—and, hopefully, to prevent—crises. What the next generation of trade surveillance and risk systems needs is a crystal ball.

Specifically, there are seven essential pillars that a next-generation smart surveillance system must have:

1. **A convergent threat system**—Banks currently utilize different systems to detect different problems. As we have seen, however, to be really smart, surveillance needs to analyze everything. The system should be able to spot rogue algorithms that are operating outside their normal behavioral patterns and shut them down. It should also identify rogue traders, market manipulators and insider dealers and alert the compliance team. The common thread in all of these scenarios is the use of smart algorithms to monitor behavioral patterns in the market. Utilizing a single framework for all of these cases will lead to reduced ownership costs, more efficient maintenance and a more informed, intelligent system.

2. **Support for historical, real-time and predictive monitoring**— Historical analysis means you find out things only after they

have happened—maybe weeks or even months later. In contrast, real-time analysis enables us find out about something as it is happening—freeing us to act quickly to mitigate its consequences. Continuous predictive analysis allows us to extrapolate what has happened up to this point. We can then predict that something might be about to happen—and prevent it! Consider a wild algorithm, as happened at Knight Capital. Under normal circumstances we can be monitoring the algorithm's operating parameters, which might include data such as which instruments are traded, the size and frequency of the orders and the order-to-trade ratio. If we become aware that the algorithm has suddenly started trading outside the "norm"—for example, placing orders far more frequently than usual without pause (a la Knight Capital)—then hopefully we have time to initiate preventive measures such as blocking the orders from hitting the market. In general, then, real-time monitoring enables us to act in time to have an impact on the business.

3. **Support for fast Big Data**—Effective surveillance often involves drinking from the fire hose of market and trade data. Monitoring fast Big Data now also includes keeping tabs on social media, emails, instant messages, news headlines and even audio data from phone calls. If chat room activity, followed by large trading activity, followed by a news item results in unusual profits, then alerts will flag management of possible insider trading. Surveillance can also be enhanced by tapping into in-house human resources data, middle- and back-office data and entry card data to identify traders who are working unusual hours, cancelling trades before settlement or never taking holidays.

4. **Support for multi- and cross-asset class monitoring**—An *asset class* is a type of instrument, like equities or futures. Few trading

houses now focus on a single asset class. Consequently, an effective surveillance system must monitor multiple asset classes for abuse. From equities and futures to oil and foreign exchange, rogue algorithms can disrupt markets. Scandals such as LIBOR, FX and alleged metals fixings provide compelling evidence that financial services firms and regulators must watch *all* markets at *all* times.

5. **Support for cross-border surveillance**—Cross-border surveillance is increasingly critical. Globalized trading means multiple regulatory regimes, creating confusion and opportunities for error or even regulatory arbitrage—where traders move to less-regulated trading environments. Regulations in different countries (e.g., Dodd-Frank in the United States and the Markets in Financial Instruments Directive, or MiFID, in Europe), although grounded in the same basic principles, can vary in their specifics. Employing a uniform system, but with appropriate flexibility for different regions, would reduce complexity and save money.

6. **Support for known and unknown threats**—Whenever I attend a conference or customer meeting that focuses on market surveillance, one theme keeps repeating. Time after time, compliance officers and other C-level executives fret about the great unknowns—those events, traders, algorithms and cyberterrorism activities that could be the Next Big Problem in capital markets. Flash crashes, fat-finger trades, insider dealing and benchmark fixing are the *known knowns*. They are frightening enough. However, it is primarily the *unknown unknowns,* to paraphrase former U.S. Secretary of State Donald Rumsfeld, that keep capital markets players and watchdogs awake at night. Regulators can monitor for unknowns by benchmarking behavior that is normal over time and then identifying behaviors that deviate from the

norm. Such monitoring may pick up behaviors that would not fall into one of our defined rules but nevertheless are outside of what could be considered normal behavior. They can be investigated in more detail and perhaps form part of a new rule.

Consider the following scenario: A trader converses via instant messaging with another trader she doesn't usually speak to, she then makes an unusually large trade in a stock she doesn't usually trade in and all of this occurs just prior to a market-moving news event that raises the value of the stock by 35 percent. In this case an effective surveillance system would raise a potential unusual behavior alert.

7. **The ability to evolve new rules at any time**—When we spot a new unknown behavior, we need to make it a known behavior by adding a new rule to the system. For example, if a trader is conversing with a previously unknown third party, an alert could be sent to compliance that could then approve or reject the third party for future reference.

Market surveillance ideally must involve watching everyone and everything at once. It means sniffing out abnormal trader behavior while, at the same time, monitoring markets for possible manipulation—and reading news headlines while checking on chat rooms for possible wrongdoing. When every possible base is covered and a system can alert compliance teams to the smallest anomaly, then we'll all sleep better.

Smart Credit Ratings Beat Expectations

Credit ratings agencies became a household name during the 2008 credit crisis—but not in a good way. A harsh spotlight was shone on the initially favorable ratings issued by Standard & Poor's, Moody's and Fitch Ratings for the subprime mortgage bonds that underpinned the U.S. housing boom of 1998–2006, along with "the self-reinforcing housing price bubble[53]."

Standard & Poor's has been around for about 150 years, but prior to the financial crisis it was really known only among financial markets participants. As S&P became more widely recognized, the firm decided to proactively meet and surpass new regulations. These rules include tighter controls on how ratings are determined as well as measures to prevent analysts from producing inflated ratings to create sales[54].

Mark DuBrock, Global Head of IT Operations for S&P, claims that ratings agencies are now as tightly regulated as banks. "There are 13 regulators globally looking at us, all with slightly different expectations, but they will keep getting stricter. We decided we are going to be the best at being regulated."

> **"We decided we are going to be the best at being regulated."**
>
> **Mark DuBrock, S&P**

Ratings are a key element of S&P's business. They indicate an entity's financial performance and credit worthiness. Creating them involves a complex business process that utilizes both human and computer algorithm activities to collect and collate all of the necessary input data.

Customers who pay to receive ratings enter into service-level agreements (SLAs) with S&P to ensure they receive this information at an appointed time. However, all sorts of issues can impact the creation of ratings: back-end system failures, human workflow failures, network failures and so on. With so many moving parts, it is easy for S&P to fail to meet their desired service levels.

---

[53] Lawrence J. White, 1 Stern, NYU: "Credit Rating Agencies and the Financial Crisis: Less Regulation of CRAs Is a Better Response." https://www.stern.nyu.edu/sites/default/files/assets/documents/con_039549.pdf

[54] Joseph Lawler, Washington Examiner, August 27, 2014: "Regulators OK overhaul of credit rating agencies." http://www.washingtonexaminer.com/regulators-ok-overhaul-of-credit-rating-agencies/article/2552504

S&P has implemented a standardized method of rating bonds. The process begins when the issuer signs a contract with S&P. It then moves through several layers of teams and committees before S&P arrives at a decision.

Each layer of the process is crucial to getting the rating completed, approved and reported. Therefore S&P wanted visibility so it could monitor exactly what was happening at each stage. That way, if something was "stuck" in one stage, management would be alerted and could take remedial action.

In 2010 S&P embarked on a project, known as RAD, to add a platform for real-time visibility and process tracking. RAD taps into the IT monitoring systems for the web, network and servers along with the business process management system. It can provide a single view of how the ratings process is progressing, and it can alert management of any developments that can impact service levels. Essentially RAD is a Thingalytics-powered RoboCop with a face.

Mark claims that although S&P built RAD as a general purpose Big Data analytics platform, the company can rapidly build any analytical apps as long as the right data streams are fed in. After S&P had achieved continuous visibility and the ability to perform continuous analytics to predict problems, Mark's team created many more killer apps that expanded the original RAD concept.

For example, they built algorithms to approximate "real-time Monte Carlo models," a complex model that identifies any emerging risks to the business. Usually such models are run in batches and are not real-time—and thus cannot show what is happening now or predict what is about to happen. In contrast, with RAD: "The more real-time and predictive the system is, the more valuable it is to the business." The result? S&P can now spot issues before they become problems. This capability reduces costs and protects the company's reputation.

That is a key principle of Thingalytics.

Conclusions

Thingalytics is not just about creating new applications like smart homes and smart transport systems. It is also about protecting us from things going wrong, sometimes in the very systems it has helped to create! Thingalytics is about policing human- and computer-driven ecosystems, checking that they stay within the law and, if necessary, taking action to ensure they do.

In this chapter we have focused primarily on financial markets as a major case study. RoboCops, however, can apply to many domains. In the city of the future, we will experience cars that communicate with a smart road network to avoid collisions, optimize routes and maintain order. Of course some naughty, tech-savvy human could tweak her car to break the speed limit.

A RoboCop road-monitoring algorithm would spot this infraction and pull her over or slow her down. Similarly, in a smart home we will be able to route power as easily as network packets and continuously buy from the cheapest provider right now. However, another tech-savvy, naughty human could reroute the power network from his neighbor's house to feed his house. A RoboCop power-monitoring algorithm would spot this setup and fine him. We have already read how S&P uses RoboCops to detect impending breaches of service levels in its rating process.

In the world of financial markets, smart trade surveillance can detect and respond immediately to dangerous market conditions. It can identify and stop fat fingers, erroneous algorithms, rogue traders and other excessive trading risk exposures. Trade surveillance involves searching trading data for behavioral patterns that indicate that a potentially abusive or dangerous incident has occurred. Continuously conducting this analysis enables us to detect potential abuse as it is happening. In some cases it can even identify abuse in its early stages. Thingalytics has enabled regulators to scrutinize data for complex patterns over time as the data is flowing in. To avoid the next flash crash and to prevent market abuse and risk-management disasters, regulators and financial services firms should be hungry for visibility, constantly monitoring positions for risk on a real-time basis and observing traders and back-office staff for anomalous behavior. Only by being vigilant can they remain smarter than—and ahead of—the average criminal.

7

Planes, Trains and Automobiles

Baby, You Can Drive My Car

Human beings are not very good drivers. We are easily distracted, and we get tired. We can drink too much or drive under the influence of both legal and illegal drugs. Some of us do not see very well in the dark. In the United States in 2012, more than 30,000 people died and 2.4 million were injured in 5.6 million motor vehicle accidents, according to the U.S. National Highway Traffic Safety Administration. We crash a lot.

These observations explain why cars are ideal candidates for Thingalytics. Cars can be sensor-enabled to detect other vehicles in our blind spots and alert us before we change lanes. Similarly, they can alert us if a car is stopped up ahead, in case we happen to be glancing at our text messages.

There are even driverless cars in the works. Google[55] has been testing a self-driving car that uses detection technologies including radar and sonar devices, stereo cameras and lasers. Audi[56] is testing a fully automated piloting system on its RS 7, which has already broken a speed record in Germany. The RS 7 uses regular in-car GPS, which is accurate to about three feet. Audi has supplemented this technology with a second system that transmits corrected GPS signals over Wi-Fi, bringing the tolerance down to an inch or so. Audi does not intend to sell a totally self-driving car. Rather, it wants to enable drivers to relax and let the car do the worrying.

I recently took delivery of a Tesla Model S, which uses long-range radar, a single forward-looking video camera and 12 ultrasonic sensors to create a 16-foot bubble around the car. In 2015, onboard Thingalytics software will become available to download to the Model S that will use these sensors

---

[55] Ryan Whitwam, Extreme Tech, September 8, 2014: "How Google's self-driving cars detect and avoid obstacles." http://www.extremetech.com/extreme/189486-how-googles-self-driving-cars-detect-and-avoid-obstacles
[56] Aaron Souppouris, Engadget, December 18, 2014: "Riding in Audi's 150MPH self-driving RS 7, the anti-Google car." http://www.engadget.com/2014/12/18/audi-self-driving-rs-7-concept-test-drive

to enable a feature called "Autopilot." With Autopilot, the Tesla can read speed limit signs and alert me if I am going too fast. In addition, it can follow lanes, turns and curves without requiring me to turn the wheel. It can even make an emergency stop when it detects looming danger!

It is not just cars that are being sensored-up for Thingalytics. Ships have the Automatic Identification Systems (AIS), airplanes have avionics, and trains sport GPS tags—all of which produce vast quantities of data with every mile they travel. Cities are being sensor-enabled to make them smarter; traffic lights can judge when traffic is heavy and change accordingly to ease blockages; parking garages can provide information on available spots to park.

Taxi services have also been revolutionized by sensors and smart apps. New services such as Uber and Lyft offer a smart phone app that allows customers to see on a map the proximity of nearby cabs and private cars for hire. This app also informs customers how long it will take for a car to get to them, so they can choose to book the car or not. Meanwhile, the car drivers use the app to accept fares and locate the passengers by utilizing the GPS sensor on their smart phones. As the car approaches, the passenger follows the car's progress on the map. This revolutionary approach improves customer satisfaction by providing full visibility of car availability while reducing costs for passengers and drivers. Drivers don't need an expensive cab license or a passenger-booking service; rather, they are matched to passengers electronically. These improvements will lower their costs. Similarly, passengers don't have to call a private cab company or struggle to flag down a taxi. Instead, they can click and watch as the cab approaches. This is a first step towards what is possible with Thingalytics.

Roads are becoming smarter, too. In fact, a solar roadway[57], which can power itself—its traffic lights, crossings and alerts—while simul-

---

[57] Teo Kermeliotis, CNN, September 18, 2014: "Solar-powered roads: Coming to a highway near you?" http://edition.cnn.com/2014/05/12/tech/solar-powered-roads-coming-highway/

taneously feeding the electricity grid may soon become a reality. Solar roadways are the invention of Scott and Julie Brusaw. The Brusaws have built prototype 12-foot by 12-foot solar panels that can bear the weight of a 250,000-pound truck. These panels slot together to create a road surface. If the entire U.S. road network were covered with solar roadway panels, it would generate 3 times the electricity currently consumed in the entire country. Another benefit of solar roadways is that they don't need to be plowed because the surface of the road heats up so the snow can simply run off. In addition, LED lights are built into the surface so the road markings can be displayed dynamically and customized to the conditions. Going further, sensors can detect changing conditions and alert drivers to them. Imagine you are driving on a foggy day and you are approaching a hill in the road. Suddenly the road surface in front of you lights up and warns you that it has detected a deer standing in the road, just over the crest of the hill. The deer and you can both breathe a sigh of relief!

At this time solar roadways are a vision of the future. However, some projects are coming to light that provide a glimpse into the possibilities. For example, the Netherlands has implemented a 70-meter (230-foot) solar bicycle path[58] between two suburbs near Amsterdam, and it is looking to extend the technology to the country's public roads.

Imagine the amount of information generated by these sensored roads, cars, planes, trains and automobiles, combined with data from smart cities. The computational explosion of data complexity is huge as objects move, come into proximity with one another and signal other conditions such as weather and the locations of roaming deer, which change continuously. If we can conquer that complexity using Thingalytics, then we can build apps that harness this rich real-time data.

---

[58] http://www.sciencealert.com/world-s-first-solar-road-opens-in-the-netherlands

For example, Thingalytics will enable me to tell my Tesla to park itself while I attend a meeting in the city. The car will be able to find the cheapest available parking within a 10-minute range of my location. Going further, I could actually earn extra money by linking up with a service such as Uber or Lyft that would employ my car as an itinerant taxi while I'm at my meeting. And then, when the meeting is over, I'll be able to call my car to come back and get me!

> **Thingalytics will enable me to tell my Tesla to park itself, finding the cheapest available parking within a 10-minute range, while I attend a meeting in the city.**

In the future, Thingalytics will enable smart cities to manage traffic jams. It will allow haulage and cargo companies to proactively manage logistics and even predict when their vehicles will need maintenance. Finally, it will provide manufacturers with unprecedented visibility into their supply chains, helping them to prevent production and transportation bottlenecks.

In sum, then, logistics and IoT are made for each other. And Thingalytics is just the matchmaker they need.

Leave the (Smart) Driving up to Us

In the 1987 film *Planes, Trains and Automobiles*, John Candy and Steve Martin take a bus as part of their epic, transportation-failure-filled journey from New York City to Chicago for Thanksgiving.

At the bus terminal Candy's cheerful character turns to Martin's grumpier one and asks: "Have you ever travelled by bus before?"

Martin says no.

Candy responds: "Your mood is probably not going to improve much."

Candy was right. Bus travel at the turn of this century was not glamorous. In contrast, back in the 1940s and 1950s, the glory days of

U.S. passenger bus travel, there was an aura of glamour and romance surrounding it. Greyhound was the epitome of elegance, with its stream-lined, Art Deco[59]-style buses and stations. Bus travel represented freedom for many people—an economical way to see America.

In the 1970s this situation began to change as people started driving their own cars or taking airplanes to travel long distances. Bus travel faded into the background and became a more utilitarian method of travel. It was identified with college students who had limited funds and people with modest incomes who could not afford a car. Greyhound, the iconic passenger bus company, aims to change this—both the perception and the reality.

Chris Boult, Chief Information Officer at Greyhound, states: "Greyhound's brand is one of the most recognized icons in the world; it is up there with the Nike 'swoosh.' But [Greyhound's] brand regard has waned since the 1960s and 70s."

Chris's boss, Greyhound President and CEO Dave Leach, has long entertained a vision to transform Greyhound back into a top-class cus-tomer experience and reinvigorate its valuable brand. Dave worked his way up in the company from a baggage handler in Edmonton, Canada.

As Chris observes: "He always had a hunger for transforming the brand and getting Greyhound back to greatness." Chris and his team are performing a vital role in this endeavor by totally rethinking technology approaches, utilizing Thingalytics to improve customer experience, avoid threats and optimize operations.

Travel is in Chris's blood. He joined British Airways when he left Lancaster University in the U.K. He then spent time at consultancy firm Accenture, where his clients included Southwest, JetBlue and AirTran airlines as well as several retail accounts. "The mixture of retail and transportation was good background for Greyhound," notes Chris.

---

[59] http://amhistory.si.edu/onthemove/exhibition/exhibition_14_3.html

A one-year contract at Sabre, the computerized reservation system division of American Airlines, took Chris to the United States, where he remains today. He first joined Greyhound in 2008, but he left in 2010 a few years after the company was acquired by the U.K. and U.S. transport operator FirstGroup.

As often happens, Chris's life direction changed. He recounts: "I got a call in May of 2013 to come back and build a Greyhound team to lead the technology transformation of the Greyhound brand."

Dave Leach's initial priority was to reinvigorate Greyhound's customer experience. He then wanted to breathe new life into the company's sustainable revenue growth and EBIT (earnings before interest and tax) performance, along with shareholder return.

"In the dark years, the mid-1980s to early 2000s, Greyhound went through two bankruptcies, and there was little investment in terminals, buses or IT. Early 2000s EBIT was less than $1 million on revenue of about $1 billion. Poor returns and little investment," notes Chris.

In the late 1990s, Greyhound was acquired by the Burlington, Ontario-based transportation conglomerate Laidlaw. Cash-strapped, the company had not bought any new buses or invested in terminals or technology in years. Laidlaw itself then declared bankruptcy in 2001.

"Greyhound had not bought any buses in 10 years; passengers had a horrible experience in terminals pre-trip, and on the buses—nearly 40 percent were breaking down mid-trip" states Chris, adding: "The data centers were true museum pieces."

When FirstGroup took over in 2007, the company needed a multiyear plan to transform the brand. First came the buses: "It's no good having great technology if your buses don't run," Chris asserts.

Greyhound had a fleet of 1,900 buses which would have cost millions of dollars to replace. So, the company embarked on a refurbishment program in which an initial 800 buses received a complete makeover, followed by a program to purchase 60–100 new buses per year. Chris claims the company is close to refreshing the entire fleet. In his words: "We now have much nicer buses; we were the first in North America to introduce Wi-Fi, leather seats and three-point seatbelts. And our reliability increased massively."

Having completed that step, Greyhound shifted its focus to utilizing the most current technologies. Chris explains: "We had new technology and capabilities with the buses that we started to hook into. We could perform remote monitoring of the engine control units and measure bus and driver performance using cameras and GPS to improve operational performance."

Greyhound can detect when buses are off-route or burning fuel unnecessarily.

Utilizing this technology, Greyhound could, for example, detect when buses were off-route or were burning fuel unnecessarily.

To quote Chris: "We found that we could save about 5 percent in fuel costs by minimizing excessive idling, particularly in Canada, where it is cold."

The second priority was to improve customer experience at the terminals. Specifically, Greyhound sought to enhance the look and feel of the terminals by offering free Wi-Fi and improving the back- and front-office technology. The company soon realized that although its legacy brand demographic includes lower-income people, students and people who are unemployed or underemployed, nearly every one of these customers carries a smart phone. "This is their Internet connection," Chris explains.

Utilizing this knowledge, Greyhound quickly built an online app for ticketing, in order to capture customer information. The app, launched in October 2014, sent sales through the roof with much of it being new business, although some sales activity essentially shifted from the traditional web to mobile. Further, when Greyhound was building the app it realized that this technology created an opportunity to sign up more loyalty members. So, the company made the mobile app experience much more pleasant if customers signed up for the loyalty program immediately. The app saves customers' trip information as well as their profiles. In this way Greyhound transformed buying tickets from a 6- or 7-click ordeal to a 1- or 2-click experience. Greyhound is now witnessing a phenomenal 5–10 percent growth *per week* of loyalty customers.

Meanwhile, Chris's colleague, Andy Kaplinsky, Greyhound's Chief Commercial Officer, was pursuing two objectives: (a) seeking a better way to sell tickets through technology and (b) engaging with customers by offering them a more personalized travel experience.

Andy explains: "The app will be able to send pop-up offers on customers' mobile phones that give them a coupon toward a burger at the next stop, for example. We know they are going to be stopping there." He continues: "Customers can order the food they'd really like in advance, and the food can be ready, as it will be linked to the arrival time of the bus, so there's no delay. This helps with streamlining logistics for both Greyhound and our customers."

Having built a Thingalytics-style platform to generate insights into the customer base, Greyhound will use the information it gathers to create real-time offers. "Previously we were not even collecting email addresses," Andy

> **Greyhound will use the Thingalytics information it gathers to create real-time offers.**

concedes. "Now we have knowledge about customers, their behavior and the logistics around the trip" to use for location-aware offers.

Another Thingalytics innovation comes from the use of semi-autonomous, or partly self-driving, vehicles. Because safety is one of Greyhound's core values, semi-autonomous buses may help to alleviate one cause of accidents—human error. For example, cameras on board can feed video into a Thingalytics platform to detect patterns that indicate a driver may be drowsy. They can then send alerts to both the driver and management, who can then decide whether to replace him. Another innovation, self-driving assistance, will prevent a bus from drifting into another lane or, worse, from hitting a stopped car in front of it.

Greyhound can also use the data generated by IoT-enabled buses to improve drivers' reliability and driving skills. As Chris observes: "We have IoT data on driver performance. Are they braking suddenly a lot? Did they have an accident? Then we can use this to coach the driver to operate better, safer."

Going further, this data can save the company money and improve their customers' experience. Chris explains: "In congested areas we can change the route, saving fuel and making the customer experience better." As one example, Greyhound's BoltBus brand is using innovative technology that monitors a bus's location, compares it to its schedule and overlays traffic information. Using historical traffic data, Greyhound can detect patterns and perform predictive analytics to help optimize routes.

The data that Greyhound is, and will be, collecting will offer some insights and even some surprises. Chris predicts: "Thingalytics will call into question some of the ways we have been running our business."

Smart Ships

When Lehman Brothers failed in September 2008 and the credit crisis and recession hit the Western Hemisphere in earnest, few people suspected that these events would cause major disruptions in shipping patterns. In fact, by November of that year Bloomberg was already reporting that ship owners had idled 20 percent of their bulk carriers. Rates had collapsed—some had plunged as much as 98 percent in five months.

According to the international law firm Ince & Co.[60], freight rates crashed at the "fastest pace ever recorded, as banks shut off credit lines

---

[60] http://whoswholegal.com/news/features/article/15859/the-credit-crunch-impact-shipping-contracts

to the industry, precipitating a sudden crunch in world trade. Freight rates have never fallen this steeply before, and it reflects the fact that trade in raw materials has slowed dramatically."

Manufacturing output shrank, leaving little merchandise for the ships to haul. Meanwhile, letters of credit—the primary method of financing—became much more difficult to obtain. Shipping lines were at risk of breaching loan accords due to their declining income. Ships were unable to find cargoes to haul, and ship owners refused to accept the lower rental rates. It was a desperate time.

A container ship can cost a huge amount to run—which is fine if it is fully loaded, but not so good if it is (say) half-loaded. A typical container ship may use 350 metric tons of fuel per day at full speed. Interestingly, at half speed it may use only 150 metric tons per day. For this reason, many shipping lines were practicing "slow steaming"—traveling at slower speeds—to consume less fuel. At the same time, however, the ships still needed to be at the right place at the right time to fulfill their service level agreements. The process of continuously adjusting speed while adhering to a schedule is a highly complex activity for a human to manage.

Because of the long distances involved, changing weather and speed adjustments, ships are often in the wrong place at the wrong time. They may arrive in port before or after their scheduled arrival time or not at all, causing a number of issues with port authorities and suppliers. Shipping is an essential component of the global supply chain. If a ship is late, parts do not get to manufacturers who are ready to assemble them into cell phones or computers or cars.

Shipping is an essential component of the global supply chain.

Fortunately, Thingalytics can help alleviate these problems. Using a Thingalytics approach, ships can add more intelligence, such as dynamically optimizing fuel usage, course and speed based on the locations of other ships, weather patterns and the availability of port berths.

Imagine that a cargo ship is headed for Rotterdam, Europe's largest port. The ship—we'll call it the *Cambridge*—is arriving almost three days early because the shipping company speeded up to pick up a new cargo after a previous contract fell through. Under ordinary circumstances this ship would have to slow down and sit outside the port because no pilots would be available. Moreover, even if a pilot could be found, the ship could be too early for its berth at the cargo handler's docks. In addition it could be low on food and fuel, in which case barges would have to be dispatched—at additional cost—to keep it provisioned. In sum, the unscheduled early arrival could cost its owners tens of thousands of dollars—possibly its entire profit margin.

Today, however, Thingalytics has dramatically reshaped this scenario. This *Cambridge* is equipped with an onboard system that informs Port of Rotterdam officials it will arrive ahead of schedule. Port management has already shifted a cargo ship off the berth that is booked for the *Cambridge,* and it has ordered a pilot to stand by. It has also alerted a ship's provisioner, which has fresh food, and a bunkering company, which is waiting with fuel. Rather than wait several days to be serviced, the *Cambridge* will be ready to go as soon as it receives another contract.

This is an example of what Thingalytics can do to keep the largest port in Europe running smoothly. The system described in the previous paragraph, which is mandatory on all ships of 300 gross tons and upwards, is called the Automatic Identification System (AIS). It was designed by the maritime information and service provider Royal Dirkzwager. AIS uses a signal from the *Cambridge's* onboard very high frequency (VHF) radio to reveal the ship's location, speed and direction.

Port authorities can utilize this information to determine where the vessel is, its approximate sailing time and at which port it is expected. Paul Wieland, Manager of Offshore & Pilotage Services at Royal Dirkzwager, explains: "The port can use AIS to determine time of arrival and compare that with the original estimated time of arrival. It informs the terminal that the event may change. The terminal can then re-plan its activities; for example, putting another ship into berth in its place."

> **Port authorities can determine where a vessel is, its approximate sailing time and at which port it is expected.**

AIS technology is critical to making the massive port run smoothly. There are hundreds of companies in and around Rotterdam that provide maintenance and repair, fuel and food provisioning, ships' management, waste disposal, cleaning, cargo inspection and myriad other services. In 2014 more than 30,000 vessels arrived from other ports, and more than 100,000 barges came up the Rhine River. Cargo throughput in Rotterdam was around 450 million metric tons. This cargo included agricultural products such as grains in addition to iron ore, scrap metals, coal, crude oil and oil-based products and even mineral oil.

Royal Dirkzwager was formed in 1872 with a simple purpose— to help people at the port find out which ships were coming in and when. The method? Standing on the shore with a pair of binoculars and scanning the horizon for ships. When a spotter saw a ship, he would jump on a horse and ride like the wind to tell whomever was interested. Paul asserts that the business plan has not changed much, but the methodology certainly has. Disseminating important port-related information evolved from horse and rider to fax and telex in the middle of the 20th century. Today it can be delivered by text messages and email.

AIS has made extensive data lists digitally available, and Royal Dirkzwager collates this data to make sense of it for its customers. The company utilizes Thingalytics to sort information such as which vessels are expected in port within the next 24 hours, which ones are currently there and which ones sailed out in the last day based on customer requirements. It can then push out alerts via SMS or email.

Paul describes this process: "Most suppliers in the port are [most] interested in which ships are expected. They are providing a service to these ships, either on contract or on-the-spot. Some are vying for their business." He continues: "We define the parameters, put them into an algorithm and analyze them against real-time data. It completely changes the way they are working. No more huge lists to go through. The company provides us with a list of ships that it is interested in. We use event-processing software and location awareness to determine when the ship enters the port. Then we alert the customer."

Royal Dirkzwager is helping the entire shipping supply chain to become more intelligent. Thingalytics enables shipping companies, ports, agents and ships' suppliers worldwide to continuously optimize their schedules and resource utilization.

Smart Trucks

In addition to cars and ships, trucking logistics applications also use GPS, along with other sensors and wireless communications, to track the location and status of trucks and to identify problems. One real example, shared with me by a provider of trucking logistics software, illustrates how a Thingalytics-style solution can detect and resolve an issue. In this scenario, by continuously monitoring and analyzing truck locations, the software detected that a particular truck driver was more frequently late with his deliveries than the average driver. Upon analyzing his routes, the trucking firm he worked for discovered that he stopped periodically at certain locations, which suggested he could be drinking in bars. A surprise alcohol test, which the driver failed, led to a swift dismissal.

Another area where location-aware applications have great potential to improve operations, reduce costs and even save lives is the military. In today's "digital battle space," or the field of "network-centric warfare" as it has been termed, all vehicles (e.g., tanks, planes and refueling tankers), military personnel and other hot zones (e.g., minefields and command-and-control posts) can be tracked. It is thus possible to roll out smart applications that can warn a squadron if they are too close to a minefield or to prevent an impending act of friendly fire when the data reveals there are allies in the zone where the military is about to attack.

Napoleon Bonaparte famously declared: "An army marches on its stomach." Without food and supplies, military operations cannot proceed. The military has one of the most complex supply chains in the world. Tracking the locations of supply vehicles and tanker trucks is critical in the digital battle space. The modern military can employ Thingalytics to optimize the deployment of these vehicles and to ensure their protection.

Smart Airlines

Modern airlines can also benefit from Thingalytics. Consider the following scenario: In 2010 the Eyjafjallajökull[61] volcano eruption in Iceland closed more than 75 percent of Europe's airspace and created the most severe global air travel disruption since the Second World War. This catastrophe stranded millions of people, some for weeks. The ash cloud chaos caused untold damage to the reputations of global airlines, airports and relevant government officials. It also opened up a can of worms for airlines as the storm of criticism veered away from the actual crisis and onto more mundane irritations, such as delays and baggage charges.

---

[61] http://en.wikipedia.org/wiki/2010_eruptions_of_Eyjafjallaj%C3%B6kull

Joshua Norrid has had a rich career in the airline industry. He served as the Senior Director of the Application and Data Architecture division at the innovative Southwest Airlines, before working with me[62]. Joshua informed me: "Even if the airlines could have predicted the ash cloud, or indeed any other serious weather issues, there would still be significant logistics problems to deal with."

Joshua describes a scenario involving a major U.S. airline: The company has to manage approximately 700 aircraft with 3,500 daily departures to 100 original destinations. It also is responsible for 10,000 crew members, 5,000 maintenance workers and 6 bases scattered throughout the country that can maintain aircraft. "With such an extensive network, if you do not have adequate automation, you are done for," Joshua asserts.

> The greatest problem created by the ash cloud was taking care of displaced passengers for extended periods of time in hotels and/or finding them alternate forms of transportation.

The greatest problem created by the ash cloud situation was taking care of displaced passengers for extended periods of time in hotels and/or finding them alternate forms of transportation such as bus and train routes that were not impacted by the volcano. "It was a tough problem in that there was simply no business continuity plan in place to cover such far-reaching circumstances," Joshua recounts. This is an opportunity for Thingalytics: Being able to map existing passenger problems to changing availability on train and bus networks, as well as the availability and prices of rooms in hotels. Smarter, joined-up travel networks are a compelling opportunity for the consumer, but also for travel firms when there is a problem, because they can dip into the network to find their passengers hotels or alternative transport.

---

[62] He now works at Apigee Corporation.

Every year 3 billion passengers use commercial aviation to reach their destinations. Consequently, when something goes horribly wrong—such as the 2010 ash cloud or, to a lesser degree, the Chilean ash cloud of 2011—then the consequences are far-reaching. Many passengers perceive air travel to be more unpleasant and less reliable than ever[63], with overcrowded skies and antiquated air traffic control technology gumming up the works. Delays can be caused by weather, crew issues, air traffic control, maintenance or the airline itself. The airlines pursue two goals that sometimes appear to be in conflict: to please shareholders by maximizing profits and to please passengers by maximizing comfort and convenience while minimizing price.

Using Thingalytics technology you can look ahead at potential delays and optimize the use of available dynamic resources to address these delays.

A particular opportunity in the application of Thingalytics technology is to look ahead at potential delays (weather, late planes, missing crew) and to optimize the use of available dynamic resources (planes, pilots, crews) to address these delays. Airlines can also use Thingalytics to proactively anticipate passenger issues and try to address them before they become a customer service issue by employing strategies such as rebooking or proactively contacting a passenger to warn them of an issue.

Driven by the goal of improving the passenger experience, the U.S. federal tarmac rules have made life more challenging for the airlines. These rules require planes to return to the gate to let passengers disembark after waiting on the tarmac to take off for three hours for domestic flights and four hours for international flights. These rules were implemented following a number of high-profile incidents in which passengers sat on

---

[63] http://www.cnbc.com/id/100622381

the tarmac for many hours. The fine for violating this rule is $27,500 per passenger, which can more than wipe out a flight's profits. Falling prey to the tarmac rule, in 2011 American Eagle was ordered to pay $900,000 for exceeding time limits on 15 separate flights in May of that year. In most cases, however, airlines take passengers back to the gate before the tarmac rule is breached.

A better scenario for both the airlines and their passengers is to utilize Thingalytics to anticipate the issues that could cause a delay. For instance, imagine a scenario in which the pilot assigned to a particular flight is currently piloting an incoming flight that will be delayed due to bad weather—so she won't arrive in time. Can the airline source another pilot from the pool of available pilots? If the flight is delayed, is the crew going to exceed their maximum mandated number of working hours and need to be replaced? If so, can the airline provision a crew from the available pool? Thingalytics can assist the airlines by predicting issues such as these and re-computing the possibilities.

Another major driver in the modern airline industry is the modernization of the fleet. New aircraft are packed full of electronic sensors, which flood airline centers worldwide with 3 to 5 times more information than in the past. To illustrate this point, consider that an Airbus A380 generates 20 terabytes of data every hour. Compounding this issue is information generated from existing systems—such as check-in, boarding and baggage systems. Most airlines continue to run legacy-heavy systems. Joshua Norrid sums up the situation this way: "Their IT is tied to managing and maintaining old war horses. And then there are external factors, such as the price of fuel, which also impacts the price of airline operations and possibly fare prices."

Airlines are questioning how responsive they can be with a new fleet generating sensor data, when they struggle to handle the existing flow of information. "They will need a massive level of integration and smart systems to analyze the data flows," Joshua maintains. Airlines need to employ Thingalytics to fuse the information streams and to monitor, analyze and act on opportunities and threats. The more data streams they can feed into a Thingalytics platform, the greater their ability to explore new apps.

Airline customer service is one area that can be dramatically improved by Thingalytics. For example, proactively contacting customers whose luggage didn't make it onto the plane to assure them that their bags will be delivered to an address of their choice could avoid much anxious waiting at the carousel and even improve passenger sentiment. Further, if the customers are frequent flyers, then the airline might even know which address to send the bags to from their itinerary.

Smart Supply Chains

If a postwar manufacturer could time-travel to a modern factory, he or she would be astonished to learn how dramatically the supply chain has changed. The traditional notion of a supply chain posited that a company should be as vertically integrated as possible, producing as much as it could in order to manufacture the end product. Anything that it could not manufacture efficiently it would purchase from a nearby firm.

In recent decades that notion has been turned on its head. Since the 1990s companies have peeled layers off of the manufacturing process, stripping it down to what they consider their core business. Whatever is not core has been given to someone else to make. This transformation has made the business of outsourcing more competitive and global, as aggressive bidders in countries such as China and India compete for contracts. The supply chain transitioned from in-house production to sourcing parts and materials from every corner of the world.

The supply chain transitioned from in-house production to sourcing parts and materials from every corner of the world.

Supply chains have been stretched to the limit due to extensive offshoring, the desire of firms to run lean "just-in-time" inventories and the unrelenting pressure to reduce costs. Add to these factors the desire to simplify supply chains by using only one or two suppliers, and it becomes clear that modern global supply chains are highly vulnerable to disruptive events. Therefore manufacturers must remain vigilant to ensure that a crisis does not spell disaster for their companies.

Just such a crisis occurred in March 2011 when a 9.0-magnitude quake hit the east coast of Japan and caused a tsunami. The death toll was immense. Adding to the heartbreaking human misery was the breakdown of a large segment of Japan's manufacturing infrastructure. Specifically, many of Japan's nuclear power plants, manufacturing facilities and chemical plants were either damaged or shut down.

Because Japan is a major provider of automobile parts and electronics, businesses that depended on these supplies for their own manufacturing operations experienced delays, disruption and even shutdowns. The global supply chain repercussions from the Japan earthquake were long-lasting and severe.

Nearly five months after the quake, Honda reported a decline of nearly 90 percent in its first-quarter (April–June) revenues, illustrating how dramatically the earthquake and tsunami had reverberated. Honda attributed this drop in revenues primarily to "the impact of the Great East Japan Earthquake... and the unfavorable foreign currency translation effects."[64] Reduced automobile production and decreased sales were exacerbated by a strong yen and higher raw material costs.

Other car manufacturers in Japan and the United States were affected when parts were not delivered. Within days, for example, General Motors had to shut down a pickup truck plant due to lack of parts. That was just the beginning. In the following weeks and months businesses

---

[64] http://www.businessinsider.com/from-icebergs-to-autos-effects-of-the-japan-earthquake-are-long-lasting-2011-8

other than automobile production and sales suffered disruptions to their supply chains.

For example, mobile phone handset maker Sony Ericsson's second-quarter 2011 results suffered because the company could not obtain necessary components from Japan. In addition, its parent company, Sony, lost money because it had to suspend manufacturing at some Japanese plants due to shortages of raw materials, components and power following the earthquake.

The earthquake and its long-lasting aftershocks to global supply chains prompted a complete reappraisal of supply chain management. One lesson manufacturers learned from the earthquake is "Don't put all your eggs in one basket." For this reason many companies are now looking to increase and diversify their supply side. These developments can make supply chains even more complex by increasing the number of events and the amounts of information that companies need to manage.

Using Thingalytics, manufacturers can model the performance of all of their suppliers in real time, over time, to spot potential disruptions in their business. If a company spots an impending problem (such as a natural disaster, strike or war) and alerts management, then it can make a business decision as to whether to hedge against the disruption by securing its supplies from a different source to—hopefully—keep the chain running smoothly. Over time manufacturers can utilize Thingalytics to improve their processes and also to identify suppliers who are consistently not delivering against key performance indicators and therefore should be replaced.

> **Over time manufacturers can utilize Thingalytics to improve their processes and identify suppliers who are consistently not delivering against key performance indicators.**

When disruptions occur, the velocity or flow of materials through the value chain is constrained or even shut down, and the supply of raw materials, production and customer fulfillment is negatively impacted. Satisfying the demands of the "I want it now" generation will prompt manufacturers to move to real-time demand fulfillment that requires them to tightly integrate their supply chains, production, logistics and marketing. To accomplish these goals, they can employ Thingalytics to optimize the supply chain by sensing demand in real time and responding appropriately, even in a crisis like an earthquake.

Conclusions

There are always blunt "static" approaches to problems in logistics, supply chains and travel; for example, canceling a flight at the last minute because the pilot is a no-show or shutting down production in a manufacturing plant because bad weather has disrupted the supply chain. However, the world has become much more sophisticated and competitive. To compete and win, firms that are involved in logistics, travel and supply chains require constant visibility to be aware of what is happening, along with decision-support systems to predict and respond in real time to both opportunities and threats.

Travel, logistics and supply chain companies must consider how to employ Thingalytics to take advantage of the Internet of Things. They are now able to tap into their customers (through social media and smart phone apps) as well as vehicle data (through onboard networked sensors) and other external data (such as weather, the price of fuel and information about their suppliers). The next step is to determine how to offer game-changing services that take advantage of this data.

The big wins come when companies can simultaneously delight customers and maximize profits. As we have seen, to accomplish these goals a business needs to consider both internal data (e.g., the locations and status of its resources) and external data (e.g., the weather, the price of commodities and the behavior of its suppliers). Companies that can employ Thingalytics to optimize their resources, taking into account external factors, and still satisfy their customers will leapfrog their competitors. This strategy might involve configuring the course and speed of ships, trucks or planes in the company's fleet to optimize fuel usage and still arrive on time. It might involve continuously looking ahead to predict

The big wins come when companies can simultaneously delight customers and maximize profits.

and avoid problems such as flight delays. Or, it might involve dynamically re-creating supply chains in response to prices, demand fluctuations or disruptions. For many companies, this will be a challenge. For the leaders, however, it will be a decade of great opportunity.

The Technology Behind Thingalytics

Thingalytics Evolves with the Internet of Things

Over the past 25 years we have witnessed the transformation of the Internet into the Internet of Things. Once the Internet captured the public's imagination, its effect was revolutionary. Suddenly you could browse the web and order a book from Amazon, to be shipped directly to your home. You could bid on just about anything on eBay or trade on the stock market with E*TRADE.

The Big Need: Supporting a new class of streaming, decision-centric application requirements

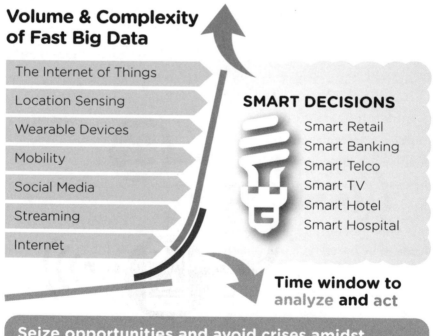

Figure 2: Drivers of Thingalytics

Today, we are witnessing the evolution of IoT due to a number of factors, as illustrated in Figure 2: streaming data, mobile devices and networks, networked sensors, wearable technologies and location-tracking capabilities. In the coming years we will be able to access a huge array of smart apps that take advantage of digitized physical world data. Smart shopping assistants will help you choose a new pair of shoes, medical monitors will send information to your doctor and smart parking apps will direct your car to the closest and cheapest garage.

Throughout this book we have discussed various apps that are utilizing this new-found capability in settings such as the supply chain, logistics and hospitals. Beyond the devices, sensors and wearables, however, what is the underlying technology that makes all of this possible? We need a platform to support Thingalytics that has the ability to integrate with the various data sources, analyze them and respond intelligently, quickly enough to have the desired business impact. Because the volume and complexity of data have expanded exponentially in recent years, a Thingalytics platform needs to be based on a completely new software architecture.

Because the volume and complexity of data have expanded exponentially in recent years, a Thingalytics platform needs to be based on a completely new software architecture.

have expanded exponentially in recent years, a Thingalytics platform needs to be based on a completely new software architecture that can handle the continuously evolving challenges.

In this chapter we explore an architectural approach to Thingalytics called "Big Data Streaming Analytics." In your organization you might structure your architecture slightly differently and achieve the same benefits. However, focusing on the principles of why Thingalytics is different from traditional database-driven apps and ensuring we address the new challenging requirements should be the key take-aways.

Computational Explosion

The new generation of intelligent applications is creating a massive scalability challenge for computing software. The problem we are dealing with is one of fast Big Data. We have *Big Data* because there is a large volume and variability of data, and *fast data* because this data comes at a high velocity, as we mentioned in the Introduction. Extracting the intelligence needed to enable a smart decision has to take place in an ever-smaller window of time.

Consider Turkcell's location-aware promotions application, introduced in Chapter 1: Turkcell's promotion decisions have to be made quickly, before the opportunity to push a location-aware offer to the customer has passed. The customer is in the right place *now*, but in a second or two he or she might have moved on!

There are millions of Turkcell subscribers walking around near Istanbul, but only a few of them will receive a narrowly targeted promotion. Nevertheless, every subscriber should be analyzed to determine whether he or she should receive this promotion, or perhaps some other promotion. The system must check each subscriber to assess whether he or she is in a relevant category, location or context to receive one of the current promotions. Adding to the challenge, this analysis is not a one-off query. Just the opposite, it must be continuous. Offers change, preferences change, people move on!

Every time one of the criteria changes, the system must recheck to identify any possible matches. For example, a subscriber who changes his or her position by a certain number of meters might have entered a 'hot zone' for a promotion. Similarly, a subscriber who uses his or her smart phone app to indicate an interest in designer clothes could become relevant for a boutique's promotion. From a different perspective, if a new promotion is made available in a particular hot zone, then it might become relevant to a set of people in that zone.

Because the relevant criteria are constantly changing, advanced systems, such as the location-aware promotions application, must operate within a *continuous query* model. Moreover, the queries must be *event-driven*; continuously monitoring, analyzing and responding to the ever-changing status of both subscribers and promotions.

> **Because the relevant criteria are constantly changing, advanced systems, such as the location-aware promotions application, must operate within a continuous query model.**

The continuous queries that determine who receives promotions are inherently multidimensional. They are made up of dimensions such as matching location, context, preferences, socioeconomic group and spending habits, and they are driven by continuous events that may update one or more of these dimensions.

For example, if a subscriber is moving, then the system needs to reassess the query in the location dimension. Keep in mind that a system with many moving objects or people creates multiple events. A thousand people moving once per minute on average translates into a thousand events per minute—around 17 events per second. For each of those events the system needs to assess whether the subscriber is currently in any of the promotion zones and, if so, whether he or she is relevant to a promotion.

The computational complexity grows rapidly as the event rates and scenario complexity increase: Sixteen times every second we have to run the equivalent of millions of traditional database queries to ascertain whether anything has changed for anyone. A million subscribers would mean a million events per minute—or 16,667 events per second. By now we would have overloaded a traditional database system—which would be so busy storing, indexing and querying data that it would, in less than a second, fall behind real time.

The same observation holds true in real-time logistics (Chapter 7), where companies are tracking large numbers of buses or ships to optimize their locations, course or speed. It also applies to capital markets trading, where large numbers of algorithms analyze potentially millions of market data events every second (introduced in Chapter 5).

In fact, there are a growing number of areas where Thingalytics needs to manage a computational explosion. As the numbers of devices and connected people continue to expand rapidly, the problem of consuming and analyzing voluminous and disparate data streams continues to balloon.

As we first mentioned in the Introduction, according to data provided by Cisco, in 2015 there are approximately 25 billion connected devices, and by 2020 the number of devices will have doubled to 50 billion. We've already seen how a popular application such as Facebook can attract over a billion users, with over 750 million using it daily[65]. As apps move towards offering Thingalytics real-time capabilities, we may see the requirement to have a Thingalytics application with 1 billion users or more before 2020. Imagine the computational complexity of billions of events per second and billions of intelligent Thingalytics scenarios analyzing and responding to patterns in the events in real-time.

Thingalytics apps need a new science underpinning them.

So, in conclusion, Thingalytics apps need a new science underpinning them. Going further, this science must be encoded into a software platform with the capacity to scale to the demands of the computational explosion. This architecture must enable modern enterprises to manage massive amounts of data that are streaming relentlessly, being analyzed continuously, learned from, personalized and acted upon!

---

[65] http://www.theguardian.com/news/datablog/2014/feb/04/facebook-in-numbers-statistics

Big Data Streaming Analytics

I have devoted a large segment of my career to researching, designing, developing and deploying technologies to drive Thingalytics apps. As an academic at Cambridge University, I developed new approaches to handle real-time sensor- and event-driven applications. I then founded the pioneering company Apama, where I took this technology into the commercial realm to assist customers who were dealing with challenging problems. From there I moved on to larger companies to combine this technology with other technologies to help resolve even more complex customer challenges. Rather than present only my viewpoint, however, I have spoken to an expert who possesses a broad perspective of the market and the associated technology challenges: Forrester Principal Analyst Mike Gualtieri.

Mike formerly worked as a software developer and development manager. Today, he spends his days analyzing, recommending and envisioning how companies should build software in the face of paradigm-shifting phenomena. Mike agrees that there is no more seismic paradigm shift than the need for Thingalytics to drive smart IoT apps.

Mike contends that Thingalytics apps are different from previous generations: "Most apps were designed for people to sit in front of them to do a task. What has changed over years is

> **"Today people increasingly expect to have their apps do what they want in context of where they are."**
> **Mike Gualtieri, Forrester**

the Internet, mobile technology and the Internet of Things. Today people increasingly expect to have their apps do what they want in context of where they are. They need real-time apps now, and these apps have to understand the environment."

Building on this observation, Mike maintains that "apps are blind, but sensors can make them see." Sensors help provide context in the form of temperature, pressure, voltage, weather and other digitized inputs. They can inform you where your customer is: At the mall? At home? Anything you can measure that is connected to the Internet can function as context. Real-time or streaming apps constantly need greater contextual awareness, which is generated by networks and sensors.

One key innovation that new software architectures have to manage is data streaming. Mike explains: "The thing is you are not asking the sensor for the data; the sensor is always reporting. Data is coming in. A traditional app is more about the request/response model. This is not streaming." When the streaming data comes in, technology has to digest the information it contains, determining what it means and whether it fits into a pattern that has business significance. Mike has concluded that a new class of application platform is necessary to perform this function.

In the 1980 movie *Altered States*, William Hurt plays a Harvard scientist who conducts experiments on himself in an isolation chamber where he deprives himself of all sensory stimuli. That is the situation with most apps today—they are blind and deaf and have no sense of smell. Clearly apps cannot reason or understand if all of their "senses" have been taken away. However, if you invest the apps with senses such as sight, hearing and the ability to detect radiation levels, they can convey richer insights than humans can. This is what it means for apps to be contextually aware.

Mike calls the new architectures required for Thingalytics "Big Data Streaming Analytics" (see Figure 3). He explains: "Most apps are request/response: They know what they want and ask for the data when they need it. Kind of like a web search. Streaming apps have to accept a constant flow of 'events.'"

Streaming Analytics technology begins with the acquisition of data. Rather than sipping data in little batches, the continuous acquisition is like drinking from a fire hose. You must connect to multiple, disparate, live data sources. Some of these sources may be your own enterprise services; some may be cloud services; some may be streaming from sensors; some could be coming from existing streams of digitized information, such as the stock market, news and weather. The app has to be able to ingest a

Driving Thingalytics with Big Data Streaming Analytics

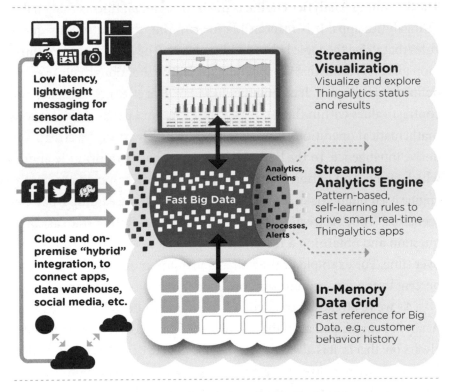

Low latency, lightweight messaging for sensor data collection

Streaming Visualization
Visualize and explore Thingalytics status and results

Fast Big Data

Analytics, Actions

Streaming Analytics Engine
Pattern-based, self-learning rules to drive smart, real-time Thingalytics apps

Processes, Alerts

Cloud and on-premise "hybrid" integration, to connect apps, data warehouse, social media, etc.

In-Memory Data Grid
Fast reference for Big Data, e.g., customer behavior history

Figure 3: Big Data Streaming Analytics Architecture

vast number of events. Moreover, the data flow from these sources may be sustained, or it may come in peaks and valleys. In the latter cases the technology must be able to handle the spikes. A Streaming Analytics engine is responsible for scrutinizing the data streams for patterns that require a response. This engine is not query-driven; rather, it is continuously "on." When it detects an actionable pattern, it can issue an alert, visualize its discovery for a human to explore or launch autonomous actions such as business processes to drive an intelligent response. To maximize their speed, Streaming Analytics architectures should incorporate in-memory rather than traditional database technologies.

The Streaming Analytics Engine

The Streaming Analytics engine is the heart of all platforms that enable Thingalytics apps. It is responsible for running the continuous query rules that drive the logic behind Thingalytics. The engine continuously monitors everything that is happening to identify situations that a user has defined as important. It can merge disparate data streams, compare and contrast values within these streams over time and perform continuous mathematical operations (the analytics) on data within the streams to derive intelligence. In the basic variant, a user has to inform the engine which events and patterns are relevant. In a more complex model, the engine itself might make some of these decisions. In Streaming Analytics scenarios, "time" is treated as a special dimension. Rather than asking a question and obtaining a result, the engine pieces together the answer over time. For example, if the voltage on a pump on an oil well rises 8 percent over a five-minute window, then it may be overheating.

As we've already discussed, a key difference between a Streaming Analytics engine and a database is that the former is event-driven and is always on; that is, it is always analyzing the data to detect patterns. Unlike a database, then, a Streaming Analytics engine can be programmed to take autonomous actions, immediately driving a decision when it detects a problem.

Mike Gualtieri has labeled the intelligence resulting from Streaming Analytics "perishable insights." The term "perishable" implies that we frequently have only a limited amount of time before the insight is no longer relevant. To react in time, the engine must have action-enabling technology as well as a data analytics system.

The action could be:

- to send an alert,
- to kick off an entire business process to drive a complex business activity,

- to make an API call into another app or to return a direct result to a user.

As these scenarios suggest, a Streaming Analytics engine must be very flexible.

Mike maintains that a Big Data Streaming Analytics engine can run a large number of streaming rules in parallel on the same data. Moreover, these rules can interact. For example, in the financial markets, as multiple transactions occur the app can filter them, enrich them and correlate patterns over time that could reflect either trading opportunities or fraud. The key point is that the engine performs all of these operations simultaneously. The ultimate objective is to act on these results, because they are usually predictive of something—whether a looming failure or an immediate opportunity.

Figure 4 illustrates an example of a Streaming Analytics rule. The scenario is a bank fraud. The engine is continuously scrutinizing customer transactions and account-closing and opening events to identify questionable patterns. In this case, if a customer withdraws more than $1,000 and then closes his account within a day, it could be fraud. According to Mike, in Streaming Analytics this kind of rule is described using "streaming operators."

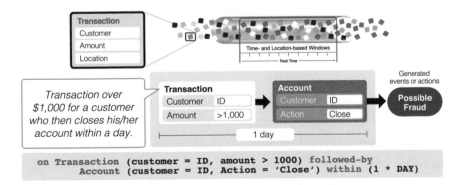

Figure 4: Example of a Streaming Analytics Rule

These operators can include:

- *Filtering*—Sieving incoming data for key items. For example, processing a stock feed and then filtering only for events pertaining to a particular stock price, let's say Tesla's stock.
- *Aggregations and correlations*—Bringing together multiple input streams and correlating on particular values. For example, discovering that a newsfeed article about Tesla was published just before the company's stock price spiked by 10 percent. The operator has aggregated the news and the stock feed using "Tesla" as the key to correlate a pattern in the two data streams.

- *Time windows and temporal patterns*—Identifying the order and timing of events. For example, alert us only if the news event about Tesla was followed within 5 minutes by an increase of greater than 10 percent in the company's stock price.

- *Location analytics*—Identifying when a particular point or zone intersects with another point or zone. For example, has a customer entered one of our stores?

- *Enrichment*—Adding data to the incoming streams to enhance their value. For example, enriching sensor IDs with the location and description of a particular sensor, so that the information is more understandable to a human when we display it in a dashboard.

Streaming operators can be used interchangeably as building blocks of more complex streaming logic; that is, a continuous query could require filtering, aggregation and temporal logic in the same scenario. Consider the following example: "Tell me when a news article comes out about any stock followed by a fall or a rise in the same stock's price of greater than

10 percent within 10 minutes of the news article." Here we see correlation (news and stock event streams), filtering (only stock events that follow news articles) and temporal logic (one following the other within 10 minutes).

Streaming Analytics engines can provide a programming language designed specifically for expressing streaming operations and associated actions. They can also provide graphical development tools that allow streaming operators to be plugged together visually. One opportunity created by this approach is to enable non-programmers to develop their own Streaming Analytics logic.

For me, the "Eureka" moment in my research on Streaming Analytics was realizing that, with the traditional query model, we store and index data and then query it when we need to. In contrast, in a Streaming Analytics world, we store and index the queries we want to look for and then stream the data through them. The queries operate like a multi-dimensional sieve, but the sieve has a memory, and it can assemble the valuable information—or the "gold nuggets"—over time.

In my approach, we built a complex multidimensional indexing technology to store streaming queries and then stream data through them. We called this technology the "hypertree." The hypertree can analyze millions of queries against millions of incoming events with sub-millisecond latency on a single CPU. Scaling hypertree-enabled analytics engines across multiple CPUs in the cloud is an exciting approach to the fast Big Data challenge. This is one approach to implementing Streaming Analytics—but of course there are others.

Fast Reference Data: In-Memory Data Grid

Another responsibility of Big Data Streaming Analytics is to cross reference historical data, so-called "reference data," with real-time data. Consider an app with a billion mobile users: How do you store all of that data? You don't want to slow down the stream, which is busy detecting patterns and taking actions on them. Plus, all of the data you need is not in that stream. You need to enrich the stream with the reference data.

To illustrate this issue, Mike Gualtieri uses a real mobile marketing app that is similar to the Turkcell and DBS apps we introduced in Chapter 1. Let's assume a mobile user is at certain mall. She is one of a million users who downloaded the app. You need the app to constantly monitor user latitude, longitude and IDs. Imagine that data is coming in continuously from a million users.

> **To make a decision, you have to translate latitude and longitude:** Is that location an area of interest? Is the customer driving nearby, or is she actually at a mall? You have to be able to look up this information. Relying on disk or database queries would be too time-consuming. You need a platform that has in-memory capability, where the data is kept in memory on site.

> **Then there is the user ID. You need the user profile to determine what to offer.** Is the user a teenager? What is the weather like? If it is a hot day and the user is a teenager, then history shows that recommending an ice cream cone will promote sales. The stream does not have the capability to analyze the reference data. And, even if it did, you do not want to slow it down.

Rather than store data on a disk—which introduces bottlenecks—you need to store it in-memory. In-memory databases and caches have dramatically improved the performance of reference data for Streaming Analytics. Of course, in-memory storage is limited by the server's memory size. To address this problem, computer scientists have devised new techniques called "distributed data grids" that enable users to manage in-memory data across multiple machines. With this technology, in-memory data caches can scale across multiple machines effectively and efficiently. We can then have the efficiency of in-memory storage and access without the size limitations of a single machine's memory capacity.

Within a big data Streaming Analytics platform, in-memory data management can be integrated with all parts of the architecture. Underpinning the Streaming Analytics engine, messaging and visualization pieces of the architecture, with an "in-memory fabric," enable much faster data storage and access and help streamline real-time processing.

Continuous Visual Feedback

Another piece of the puzzle is real-time "visual analytics," which involves continuously updating visual dashboards. We want to visualize our business or a domain in real time so we can obtain immediate insight to select an action that can avoid risk or seize an opportunity. Sometimes a human makes these decisions. In these scenarios he or she can be assisted by a visualization platform, which functions as a command center. The visual analytics component may rely on the analytics engine to provide it with information that is prefiltered and enriched so it can be visualized.

In some cases, the platform will simply visualize alerts; for example, incidents of potential rogue trading or market abuse. However, it can also visualize an entire series of event information to enable a human to "drill down" or study a visualized timeline to determine the causal relationships among the events. For instance, the platform can overlay the rogue trading events onto an event timeline, highlighting market events and identifying the root causes of the alert—news items, trades, and similar phenomena. This type of dashboard frequently would be integrated with other components; for example, the rogue trading alert could initiate a workflow rule to follow up on the alert. Part of the workflow could involve a member of the compliance team using visual analytics to drill down into the underlying circumstances.

Fast Big Data Acquisition and Integration

Thingalytics is only as good as the quality and freshness of the data that is being analyzed. High-performance messaging and integration always should underpin a Big Data Streaming Analytics platform. Going further, this integration should support plugging into a wide range of systems, collecting real-time updates and communicating the results. Existing enterprises are awash with data, much of it already connected to messaging buses that ship data between applications. So, there is already much out there to tap into.

As Mike Gualtieri observes: "While Streaming Analytics is a new way to write apps, it fits well into existing enterprises, which are flush with data. Connections to other platforms are all standard, and you do not have to reengineer other platforms. You can drop in and use existing apps as sources."

Streaming Analytics requires a highly scalable messaging architecture to stream in real-time events; to support communication among multiple streaming engines, in-memory caches and visual dashboards; and to communicate events out to applications and processes. This architecture requires adapters to connect to common APIs—such as machine-to-machine connectivity protocol (MQTT)—for collecting machine data and also to Twitter for monitoring social media data. Significantly, some applications might function as both sources and destinations of data. For example, a customer relationship management (CRM) system can be queried for customer data (source) and then updated as new customer data is created (destination).

Some of these applications could be located on the premises; for example, the enterprise software provider SAP offers an ERP application that is largely deployed on premise. Others could be situated in the cloud; for example, the cloud computing firm Salesforce.com supplies a CRM system that is available only in the cloud. An integration platform must support connectors to these and numerous other common APIs. API and graphical tools are required to manage connections to end points within the platform.

Big Data Streaming Analytics is not a replacement for existing analytics. In fact, it can be used complementarily alongside data warehouses, predictive analytics and Hadoop. To borrow Mike's terminology: "at-rest" (historical data) analytics interact well with "in-motion" (streaming) analytics. Historical analytics utilizes past data to try to predict what will happen in the future—be it an opportunity or a threat. For example, a customer who buys lemons and eggs is 50 percent more likely to buy champagne (to go with the lemon meringue pie!). The more time we have to respond to these scenarios, the better off we are. In many cases, however, we don't have much time. Rather, we have a millisecond, a second, or, at best, a few minutes.

If we can load these scenarios into a Streaming Analytics software platform, watch for them and take immediate action when they occur, then we can operationalize them; that is, we can monitor the data for the predicted conditions and react when they occur. For example, video analytics in our supermarket could track a customer who is buying eggs and lemons and then push her a coupon for a "3 bottles for the price of 2" offer on champagne to try to seal the deal.

Similarly, we might add all of the real-time analytics generated by the Streaming Analytics engine to a data warehouse or a Hadoop cluster for later analysis. Again quoting Mike: "It is wise to say that sometimes data out can be very transformative, it can create derived analytics to be poured into a data warehouse for at-rest analytics, developed for future use while at same time taking actions."

Great Answer! What's the Question?

I am proud to have contributed to the "birth" of Big Data Streaming Analytics, and I have collaborated with a lot of customers to resolve a number of fascinating problems. In some cases, these customers knew exactly what they wanted from their data. A good example is capital markets trading, where practitioners want to win and are always looking for a more effective strategy to come out on top. In other cases, even when customers are informed they can use Streaming Analytics to identify up-sell opportunities or fraud in real-time, they respond: "That sounds great, but I don't know what I'm looking for."

Recall from Chapter 2 that in *The Hitchhikers Guide to the Galaxy*, the computer Deep Thought took 7.5 million years to calculate that the ultimate answer to Life, the Universe and Everything was 42. The reason this answer was not very useful is because the people asking did not know what the ultimate question to Life, the Universe and Everything was. Thus, a new computer was created (the Earth) to calculate the ultimate question. This is the next phase for Streaming Analytics: not just being able to find the answer, but being able to ask the right questions. It is about machines learning and suggesting what might be relevant to a business. In addition to finding the "known knowns," Streaming Analytics might be able to find the "unknown unknowns."

One area in which crafting questions has been deeply explored is fraud detection. Whether in credit cards and banking, casinos or capital markets trading, fraud is a continuously evolving phenomenon. New types of fraudulent behavior are emerging all the time, and spotting these patterns is a major challenge. Compounding this problem, by the time a firm becomes aware of fraud, it could have sustained serious financial losses.

> **New types of fraudulent behavior are emerging all the time, and spotting these patterns is a major challenge.**

One approach that is being employed successfully to find these unknowns is machine learning related to "normality." Consider the scenario we introduced in Chapter 7 around detecting market abuse and rogue trading in the capital markets. Financial institutions have discovered that they can benchmark "normality" by analyzing trader behavior data over (say) six months, focusing on such factors as:

- When traders come in to work
- When they go home
- When they take holidays
- Whom they communicate with on messaging networks
- Which instruments they typically trade
- Which quantities they trade
- When they usually trade

These institutions can utilize this approach to gather and continuously refine information on a range of behaviors for all of the traders. They can then continuously monitor for major deviations to these behavior patterns by individual traders. An example is detecting that a trader has completed an unusually large trade in an instrument in which he doesn't usually trade just before a news article moved the market in that instrument by 30 percent in his favor. Is this insider knowledge or simply insight? We can drill down and learn that this trade was preceded by an unusual messaging exchange with a trader from another firm. Moreover, this scenario had occurred three times in the previous month with a similar result. Clearly this scenario cries out for further investigation.

The technology involved here is one application of machine learning, which will continue to evolve. Users will be presented with recommendations for new rules based on observed behaviors. The human becomes the expert, validating (or not) the suggested rules. The Streaming Analytics algorithms become the researchers—scanning the data for interesting new phenomena.

Another approach to adapting to current circumstances without knowing all the answers up-front is genetic algorithms, as we introduced in Chapter 6. With this approach, large numbers of algorithms are run, each one representing a different permutation of possible behaviors. In the example earlier, trading strategies are tuned by looking for which algorithm is the most profitable in its simulated trading and then using it in live trading. When it is detected that the algorithm is becoming less effective it can be replaced. A genetic-tuning framework can be developed to manage the creation, selection, evolution and deactivation of algorithms. In this way, new strategies can be evolved from what works best in the current circumstances.

There are many types of machine-learning algorithm that can be employed in a Thingalytics platform. These developments can only be highly useful, however, if there is sufficient data underlying them. If you don't capture the data or if there aren't enough data points, then it is difficult to learn. As Mike Gualtieri maintains: "You need it to happen on a regular basis for a predictive model to appear."

Life in the Cloud

In Chapter 1 we discussed an application that enables users employing wearable devices to receive an enriched augmented reality experience as they move around the world. The back-end Thingalytics capabilities run on a server somewhere, utilizing one or more central processing unit (CPU) cores. As the data loads of such an application ebb and flow, due to factors such as user behavior and time of day, the underlying hardware requirements change in tandem. Handling the load of user activity for this app in the United States at 1pm EST requires 100 CPU cores. In contrast, managing this usage load at 2am requires only 2 CPU cores.

The optimal strategy to navigate these peaks and troughs is for the platform to run in a cloud with the ability to provision computing resources automatically in response to the changing load. Some applications already operate this way, and many more will follow in the coming years.

The natural model for a large Streaming Analytics deployment is for the back-end platform to run in the cloud while at least some of the front-end capabilities run on mobile devices. For instance, a loyalty app running on a user's smart phone could transmit location and preference events to the back-end system. Within the back-end system, the analytics involved in matching offers to users occurs. Similarly, events can be collected from industrial machine sensors and sent to back-end systems for analysis. Rather than connecting to every machine directly, some companies, like the cloud service company Axeda (acquired by PTC in 2014), have created "machine clouds" that manage the collection of sensor events from machines for their customers. The machine cloud can then stream the events to analytic engines. This arrangement can simplify the collection of sensor data because it enables a Streaming Analytics platform to collect data from a single source rather than from multiple sources.

In the coming years, more and more Streaming Analytics platforms, along with the data they analyze, will be located in the cloud. To quote Mike Gualtieri: "There is lots of data that is cloud born. The cloud is where lot of processing will take place as well. All the smarts are going to be in the cloud." These platforms will utilize lightweight mobile apps as the front-end, combined with fewer on-premise deployments, as the economics of pay-as-you-use computing become more compelling.

Conclusions

The computationally explosive nature of Thingalytics requires a new kind of software platform to support the cool apps that are revolutionizing the world. This explosion arises from the massive volumes of fast Big Data that have to be analyzed against millions or billions of concurrent continuous queries and responded to in time to make a difference. A new software approach, Big Data Streaming Analytics platforms, is being deployed to address this need.

At the heart of Big Data Streaming Analytics is a real-time analytics engine. This engine sieves the data items one at a time and compares each one against active queries to determine whether it will have any impact. The engine can then raise an alert, update a dashboard, send a message or initiate an action. Patterns to scan for can be described using "streaming operators" that can join, enrich, filter and correlate patterns in multiple data streams. Streaming Analytics engines can bring predictive models to life and can even self-learn.

Big Data Streaming Analytics also requires flexible and high-performance integration and messaging platforms—to bring the data in and communicate the responses out. Real-time visualization frequently is helpful in identifying which patterns are being tracked and which decisions have been made. Streaming Analytics engines typically incorporate in-memory computing techniques both to store reference and working data in memory and to remove the traditional bottleneck of disk storage.

Streaming Analytics must be able to run in the cloud and incorporate techniques for scaling up and down, depending on the required load. This capability enables us to optimize the use of hardware resources and minimize costs, while dynamically managing spikes in the load.

> Streaming Analytics must be able to run in the Cloud and incorporate techniques for scaling up and down, depending on the required load.

Big Data Streaming Analytics is a novel approach, and it will take off more readily if it can plug into and augment existing environments. It needs the capacity to tap into data flows, sensors and applications and augment them with new easy-to-access capabilities. Many pioneering firms have achieved amazing results utilizing some or all of the techniques described in this chapter. And this is just the start!

Mike Gualtieri sums it up well: "In 2014 only 21 percent of companies were using Big Data Streaming Analytics. That is a 61 percent increase from 2012 to 2014, but still low considering the benefits. There is growing momentum, but still a minority of companies are doing this. This is perfect for the companies doing it, as it means they are first movers. In a 'winner take all' world, harnessing streaming can be the winning opportunity."

I agree with Mike that if you are one of those first movers with Thingalytics you can transform the way you are doing business with customers. Mike adds: "When Bill Gates wrote *Business @ the Speed of Thought*, things were so slow compared to now. Now we're really realizing the things Gates wrote about. And things are getting faster. This is the age of the machine things, and I love this. There is a pace at which humans can go because biology governs. But machines? The pace is faster and increasing, with more machines talking to one another, and this causes even greater demand for Streaming Analytics."

In 10 years' time, enterprise software architectures will look very different than they do today. Streaming Analytics techniques will move from the edge of systems to the very heart of systems as the world realizes that Thingalytics is essential to many businesses' survival and it offers a chance to radically improve their competitive position.

Go Forth and Use Thingalytics!

Small Changes, Big Results

Thingalytics is about a lot of small, continuous adjustments that can improve the world. It is a big deal and, as we have seen in a number of use cases, it is already changing the game in business, medicine and the home.

Thingalytics is not about long, drawn-out analysis intended to improve performance over weeks, months or years. Rather, it is about spotting what is happening now, or what might be about to happen, and using intelligence about what we have learned to improve the situation. With Thingalytics we can continuously look for and take advantage of "in-the-moment" opportunities to improve an organization's performance. Similarly, we can spot impending threats and deal with them proactively or even avert them.

There are many ways to achieve the benefits of Thingalytics. Although we explored some technology approaches in Chapter 8, my aim in this book is to draw out some of the principles and lessons that will change your perceptions of how smart systems could impact your organization. In this concluding chapter I bring together some of these lessons in an actionable prescription, with suggested next steps to apply Thingalytics in your organization.

Thingalytics Has Measurable Benefits

We discussed some of the benefits of Thingalytics in the Introduction. Now that we have explored some real-world examples and visions for the future, let's review the benefits:

> **> Optimizing operations to increase efficiency**

  - Identifying opportunities to adjust the course and speed of a ship (e.g., Royal Dirkzwager), bus (e.g., Greyhound), truck or other vehicle can reduce fuel usage, leading to reduced costs and a smaller carbon footprint. Using fewer vehicles more efficiently and identifying vehicles that are idling unnecessarily can achieve the same positive results.

- Adjusting machines' parameters based on changing real-time conditions can also reduce costs. Examples are adjusting power-generation levels (e.g., GE) based on energy-utilization demands and automatically adjusting the heat level in the house based on learned patterns about the family's habits.

- In a complex supply chain, improving the ability to keep track of key items can save time and money. Asking all tagged items (e.g., Coca-Cola coolers equipped with smart tags) to identify themselves at a particular location is much more efficient and cost-effective than finding these items manually.

- In a hospital, being continuously aware of the locations of doctors, nurses and patients, as well as current health situations, allows each doctor to be matched to the appropriate medical crisis automatically. In this way, Thingalytics can help the hospital to optimize its operations and do more with fewer staff.

> Avoiding threats

- By monitoring sensor data from industrial and retail machines as well as home appliances (e.g., GE, Coke, Electrolux), we can predict when a part will fail. We can then avert that threat, with its associated delays, costs and customer dissatisfaction, and fix the problem proactively.

- Analyzing trader and algorithm behaviors in capital markets trading firms and identifying impending threats can prevent fines, avoid trading losses and preserve a firm's reputation. Sieving fast Big Data streams for incidents such as market manipulation, insider trading and out-of-control algorithms can enable firms to address these issues before they become a problem.

- A smart hospital can prevent the spread of infections by detecting when employees have failed to observe proper precautions, such as hand sanitization, and alert people in the vicinity before anybody or anything becomes contaminated. Similarly it can detect and correlate patterns across multiple vital signs readings that might indicate an impending problem, such as a drug interaction. This technology is much more valuable to a clinician and is more likely to prevent a serious situation than traditional alarms.

- An intelligent bus (e.g., Greyhound) might be able to identify and avoid an impending crisis by analyzing video from its front and rear cameras and comparing this data to known threat situations. In the future, a solar roadway could detect a danger on the road—for example, a deer crossing—and light up the road to alert an approaching driver.

> ## Seizing opportunities to increase revenue

- Smart banks (e.g., DBS), telecommunications providers (e.g., Turkcell), retailers and hotels are pushing highly targeted, personalized marketing offers to the smart phones of mobile customers in the right place at the right time. Customers are much more likely to respond to these offers than to ads that are less targeted and are not sent in real time. Some organizations that have utilized Thingalytics have experienced a tenfold increase in offer take-up rates.

- Use of smart sensory techniques, such as video analytics, is enabling smart retailers and advertisers to identify their customers' gender, age and emotions. This information, combined with digital signage, enables retailers and other advertisers to push much more targeted ads and offers to consumers in stores and banks, or simply on the street. Retailers can employ these techniques to bring predictive buying models to life and highlight up-sell opportunities to relevant consumers right now.

- Capital markets firms (e.g., ANZ Bank and Relative Technology) are using algorithmic and high-frequency trading (HFT) techniques to identify the most profitable trading opportunities and move on them in microseconds.

- By monitoring machine usage (e.g., GE), smart algorithms can detect when an up-sell opportunity for more capacity exists. For example, if a factory is running its power-generation engine at full capacity most of the time, then it could be the right time to send in the sales team to sell an upgrade, armed with the relevant statistics.

- Vending machines that can tell you that they are nearby and have your favorite beverage (e.g., Coca-Cola) are more likely to generate sales.

> **Supercharging the customer experience**

- Receiving personalized, location-sensitive offers from a "personal concierge" (e.g., DBS, Turkcell), without feeling spammed, often increases customer loyalty.

- Smart organizations are identifying when their customers are having a negative experience and are addressing these situations proactively to enhance customer loyalty. For example, hotels that identify Diamond-tier loyalty customers who have been waiting to check in for more than 10 minutes can arrange to have someone greet and assist them. Similarly, theme parks (e.g., Disney) can enable guests to avoid excessive queuing for rides.

- Organizations are using smart algorithms fed by fast Big Data to enhance their recommendations. For example, media companies (e.g., Cox Communications) can personalize recommendations for shows their customers might like and can also ensure advertisers that they can reach the relevant demographic based on who is watching right now. The customer is happier, and so is the advertiser.

- As described above, predictive maintenance for industrial, retail and domestic machines (e.g., GE, Coke, Electrolux) enables companies to fix problems before they cause damage. The benefits include limited downtime, reduced maintenance expenses and less time wasted waiting for the repair crew to diagnose the problem. The result: massive improvement in customer satisfaction.

- Providing smart appliances in homes can improve customer satisfaction, particularly if a terrible cook can suddenly host a successful dinner party. He could download Gordon Ramsey's recipe for roast prime rib of beef with roast potatoes straight into his intelligent range and let the oven do the work.

- Travelers will enjoy a better experience thanks to real-time visibility about their journey and location coupled with context-aware offers that arrive in real time. As one example, a bus company (e.g., Greyhound) can alert passengers via a smart phone app that their bus has a stopover in 20 minutes and allow them to order from the menu through their devices. The passengers get the food they want when they want it while also saving time.

- An artificial pancreas (e.g., Medtronic) that can be implanted, analyze insulin levels and trigger an inbuilt pump can enhance the quality of life for people with diabetes. This technology is much less disruptive than continually pricking your finger, manually testing and injecting yourself.

A Prescription for Thingalytics

We have explored a number of game-changing ideas that can be achieved by *thinking Thingalytics*! We have also considered a number of real projects that are starting to bring Thingalytics into the world, harnessing data from the Internet of Things and making smart decisions to drive new benefits. So, what lessons can we extract from these projects?

You need to start thinking Thingalytics soon, or you might be trumped by your competitors—so it is critical to start. Here is a set of steps to get you started thinking Thingalytics:

1. **Do not over-analyze:** Projects that begin by trying to come up with the perfect idea rarely work. One common theme throughout the real-world examples presented in this book is that the teams come up with ideas and try them. They do not know in advance what will work. Sometimes the killer apps come from the most unexpected directions. Remember: Don't boil the entire ocean. Instead, start with a thimble of water, and go from there.

2. **Align the business and IT groups around Thingalytics:** Thingalytics is where IT and business meet. It involves collecting data from the Internet of Things, conducting analytics and taking smart actions. It is the perfect forum to bring together IT to support the business and for the business to understand what is technically possible.

3. **Create a "Thingalytics Tiger Team":** Include relevant representatives from business and IT, and appoint a visionary leader who can "get stuff done." Set aggressive goals to hear the proposals and to get the first apps into a pilot stage.

4. **Brainstorm Thingalytics scenarios:** Conduct open discussions about what you can do to supercharge your organization with Thingalytics. In your brainstorming consider how the various benefits of Thingalytics could apply to your organization. If the answers to any of the questions below are "yes," then write down the scenarios that apply, and identify the measureable benefits. Prioritize the ideas in terms of their business value.

   • Are there ways you could spot opportunities to optimize in the moment?
   • Are there threats that you could detect and avoid?
   • Are there revenue opportunities you could identify and seize?
   • Are there ways in which your customers are becoming frustrated? If so, then could you detect and avoid this problem? Better yet, could you transform this problem into a competitive advantage?

5. **Think about data:** Capturing and integrating the data to analyze is often the biggest challenge in Thingalytics. Make the most of

what you already have, and use the simplest methods to acquire what you need. Consider the following in your assessment:

- What data about Things do you already have? What does it tell you?
- What data about Things don't you have but would like to have? How could you get it? How expensive and complicated would it be to obtain it?
- Do you have sensors to digitize and capture data? Do you need to add sensors? If so, then how expensive and complicated would this process be? Are there quick solutions? Can third-party specialist organizations help you?

6. **Ensure that your thinking is fully Thingalytics:** To accomplish this task, make certain that your brainstorming is taking proper considerations of the 10 dimensions of Thingalytics:

    i. **Big Data: In motion and at rest**—Are you thinking about your data deeply enough? Are you capturing digitized data in your business to learn from? Are you comparing data in motion against data at rest to detect outliers, opportunities and threats? Are you considering what types of data are available and how your business can utilize them: social media, sensor data, video data, audio data, news data, stock data, weather data, customer behavior data and so on? The list is endless.

    ii. **Data analytics: Historic, real-time, predictive, visual**—Are you taking full advantage of the dimensions of analytics? Are you building predictive models of how to respond to various scenarios and then using real-time analytics to detect when one of these scenarios actually occurs? Are you visualizing what is happening to explore when something good or bad happens? For example, you could highlight the departments of your business on a heatmap ranging in color from green (performing great) to red (needs attention).

iii. **Media analytics: Text, video, audio, location, social**—Could you identify killer opportunities by analyzing text, video, audio, social media and location data? Recall the use-case of the supermarket that analyzes video to understand customer demographics and changes signs to encourage buyer behavior. You might think up a similar game changer.

iv. **Intelligent real-time response**—Analytics are only half of the equation. You need to be thinking about how to respond when your analytics detects something interesting. Are you still thinking batch mode (collecting and storing data), or have you freed your mind to think about real-time response? Remember: Real-time responses are critical to Thingalytics.

v. **Mobile**—Are you properly considering mobility? Your customers may be mobile—how are you providing them with information and tracking their status? Your supply chain is full of mobile objects and people—how are you handling this reality? Are you thinking "mobile first" in the design of your app so it runs natively on tablets and smart phones?

vi. **Location-aware**—Making apps location-aware is a key opportunity. How are you taking advantage of this technology? As a retailer are you pushing offers to customers when they are near your store? As an operator of heavy machinery, could you save time and money by enabling maintenance staff to get current status information on their tablet about a machine or vehicle as they approach it? The possibilities are endless.

vii. **Context-aware**—Are you considering the different states your Things move through and how your app should respond at each stage? For example, a customer might welcome restaurant offers on the weekends but block them during the work week. An intelligent Thingalytics app should understand context and adjust accordingly.

viii. **Social**—Social media has changed everything. Are you properly considering its impact? Are you analyzing your customers' responses, detecting both positive and negative feedback and responding proactively? Are you aggregating comments and measuring popular sentiments concerning your organization? Are you integrating user feedback into your Thingalytics service?

ix. **Cloud**—Are you thinking "cloud first" rather than restricting your thinking to a traditional "on-premise" model? Which cloud services can you take advantage of to "compose" your Thingalytics service? Should your apps be based in the cloud? How might the load on your app ebb and flow over time, and how would this activity translate to the needs of a scalable cloud deployment? The cloud can significantly speed up the development of new apps and make them more flexible to deploy—so it is worth incorporating this possibility into your thinking.

x. **Self-learning/continuous improvement**—How should your app self-evolve over time based on how it is used? Consider, for example, a fraud platform that records usual behaviors, spots deviations from these behaviors, flags them and then adds that behavior to the known fraud list if fraud is confirmed. Which data do we need to record, and which machine learning or feedback algorithms might we utilize and evolve?

7. **Deploy a Thingalytics platform:** A lesson you can learn from the real-world case studies is that modern businesses need a platform that allows them to explore different Thingalytics apps. This platform provides a number of general capabilities, and it enables the business to prototype new apps and then evolve them quickly. You may already have some components or even all of a Thingalytics platform. The platform must have the capacity to manage data capture, integration, Big Data analytics and intelligent response. Chapter 8 introduced a technology platform approach you can use as a model.

8. **Pilot apps as quickly as possible:** Rather than wait for perfection, get your apps out to real users as soon as possible. This process may involve a pilot project; for example, on one bus route or implemented in a single store. If you adopt this approach, then it is critical that your users understand that they are signing up for a pilot and that you value their feedback. Make certain the app is compelling and fun.

9. **Measure everything:** Record and analyze all usage data. You might find interesting patterns that tell you something. You will certainly learn whether your assumptions were correct. Use visualization to display the data in a way that a human would see visual patterns. For example, organizations that launch real-time, location-based marketing campaigns can observe in real time how effective their campaigns are second-by-second. They can then utilize this data to adjust the campaigns if necessary.

10. **Evolve apps quickly:** As you learn what does and does not work for your business, make changes. Launch new apps, and test them. Evolve existing apps. Continuously measure, learn and refine.

11. **Place algorithmic safety nets around potential threats:** If there is a circumstance in which an algorithm could cause damage, ensure that you are protected. For example, you do not want to annoy customers by sending them 10,000 offers a second because an app gets stuck in an infinite loop. Knight Capital illustrated what kinds of damage a stuck trading algo can cause. Make certain you have an algorithmic safety net that monitors critical algos, spots behavior outside the norm and shuts down malfunctioning algos.

If you follow this prescription, then I am certain you will end up with some amazing, game-changing projects. I look forward to hearing about them.

Have Fun with Thingalytics!

I never fail to get excited about the possibilities of Thingalytics, even after many years of pioneering in this space. Wherever I go and whomever I speak to, I see other people getting really excited, too. I have seen the most boring, dry IT executive crack a smile and enthuse about the possibilities. Similarly I have seen CEOs who normally focus only on the high-level details of a business get excited by a Thingalytics app that is delivering a unique capability to their customers.

> I never fail to get excited about the possibilities of Thingalytics, even after many years of pioneering in this space.

Yes, Thingalytics is fun. And it is a fusion approach. By definition it aggregates data from multiple sources to perform analytics and make decisions. It also brings together IT and business groups to discuss exciting new possibilities.

You will enjoy Thingalytics. Just remember to dive in and focus on the possible apps and their impacts. Don't get bogged down in "why this could never work." Start with what you can do, and then make pragmatic decisions as to how you could get a test-bed up and running as quickly as possible. It is likely that your initial ideas will not be the killer apps. However, the longer it takes you to try out your ideas, the longer it will take to identify the killer apps. Remember, your competitors are doing this, too—so move swiftly and with purpose. I wish you fun and success in your exploration of Thingalytics!

Acknowledgments

My book development assistant Melanie Wold is a wonderful researcher, writer and constructive critic. Mel is wonderful to work with and deserves special thanks.

My book project manager and slave driver, Lord John Stewart, also requires a special mention for his blend of insight and encouragement.

Many thanks to my editor, Robert Weiss, for his most thorough editing and useful suggestions.

My colleagues Felix Friedrich and Isabella Holst have been most helpful in getting this book published, ensuring all of the details are covered splendidly.

I'm grateful also to Luke Johnson for his wonderful artwork on the cover and inside the book.

This book would not have been possible without the vision and real world implementation of the following innovators: Ozlem Demirboga, David Backley, Audi Lucas, Kevin Flowers, Bruce Beeco, Jakob From, Paul Thompson, Hugh McGuire, Luke Marriot, Scott O'Malia, Mark Hope, Mark DuBrock, Chris Boult, Paul Wieland, Joshua Norrid and Mike Gualtieri. I wish to thank all of them for spending their valuable time with me and for their inspiration.

About the Author

Dr. John Bates is a pioneer in the fields of the Internet of Things and Big Data Streaming Analytics and is widely recognized as being one of technology's foremost innovators. *Wall Street and Technology* named John as one of the top ten "Innovators of the Decade" in 2011 and *Institutional Investor* listed him as one of the "Tech 50" most influential technologists in 2011, 2012, 2013 and 2014.

John's fascination with Thingalytics began while he was working on a PhD at Cambridge University in England. This was where he was inspired to develop the technology that would one day help businesses to run smarter.

Cambridge is an energizing environment for an academic; rich with innovative genius. Each morning on his way to the Computer Laboratory, John passed the site of Isaac Newton's physics laboratory. The university's computer lab was next to the original Cavendish Laboratory where the atom was split by Ernest Rutherford and his team in 1932.

After a hard day at the lab, John and his fellow students would often go for a pint at the Eagle pub, where James D. Watson and Francis Crick announced in 1953 that they had discovered the "secret of life" with their proposal for the structure of DNA. On their way home, John and his friends occasionally saw Professor Stephen Hawking trundling down the street in his wheelchair.

After John gained his PhD at Cambridge University he became a Cambridge academic, leading a small research group where he stumbled onto an idea that has evolved into what has been called the "new physics of computing." The idea was driven by the observation that businesses were undergoing a fundamental change—moving from a passive, data collection world to a 24 × 7, always-on, event-driven world. He knew that this new world would require businesses to interpret the real-time data, or events, which flow through the business; discovering key patterns and then responding to them proactively.

In the early 1990s, the notion of an event in computing was confined to operating systems and control systems, but this new way of thinking elevated the event to a business level concept—exposing events as "first class citizens" in the world of applications and business processes.

There was no technology that supported describing and handling patterns of events at a business level, so John and his colleagues designed and built it themselves. They designed new algorithms, data structures, techniques and architectures to enable complex event processing systems that could be constructed quickly and easily in order to support the needs of modern business. This spawned a whole new field of software.

Other researchers, such as David Luckham at Stanford University and Mani Chandy of Caltech, were coming to similar conclusions. The field ended up being called Complex Event Processing, an ironic name for something that actually makes it simple to be able to respond to patterns in events as they happen.

John co-founded a company, called Apama, with his friend Dr. Giles Nelson with the goal of capitalizing on this new science by helping companies to handle the emerging challenges. Initially they focused on addressing some burning issues in the financial services industry—algorithmic and high frequency trading—which became the first niche market for Apama. As time went on and the data deluge increased, more and more businesses began showing an interest in Apama's unique offering.

Since Apama, John has served as CTO of Progress Software and most recently CTO of Big Data, CMO and Head of Industry Solutions at Software AG. John is also a member of the Advisory Board of C5 Capital.

John features widely in industry and national newspapers and magazines, in industry-recognized blogs and has appeared on television and in video blogs. He has been profiled by the *Boston Business Journal* and quoted on the BBC's website, *The Atlantic, Bloomberg News,* the *Financial Times, Forbes, Fortune,* the *New York Times, USA Today* and the *Wall Street Journal.* He is also a regular contributor to the Huffington Post.

He is frequently quoted in trade press including ZDNet, *Information Age, Inside Market Data, Waters, Investor's Business Daily, Wall Street & Technology, Markets Media* and *Wall Street Letter.* He has appeared on CNBC, CNN, Fox Business News and Sky News.

In July 2010, John became a member of the newly established Technology Advisory Committee (TAC) for the US Commodity Futures Trading Commission (CFTC), the independent agency that regulates commodity futures and options markets in the United States.

John has long had a passion for helping businesses, from pioneering and commercializing new science and techniques from the research lab, to becoming a trusted advisor to major corporations.